Real Estate Investing:

The Ultimate Practical Guide To

Making your Riches, Retiring

Early and Building Passive Income

with Rental Properties, Flipping

Houses, Commercial and

Residential Real Estate

By Victor Adams

Table of Contents

Chapter One: Introduction

At the young age of 29, while others were buried in student debt and dead-end jobs, Kris Burns, a self-made real estate investor who started off with no capital funding now feels like he can breathe with ease and anticipate a bright future ahead. It has taken him four years to get to this position.

He's driving his dream car, traveling the world and has finally managed to hire a personal trainer to help him shed some of the extra weight that used to make him feel self-conscious. Best of all, the girl of his dreams just said yes, and they are planning a wedding for next fall. Life is beautiful in Kris's world.

But the path to this point hasn't been easy. Not too long ago he was crippled by student debt. He had a Masters degree, but no hope for a high paying flexible job and no money in the bank. This isn't a unique case.

Many well-educated men and women find themselves stuck in a life that feels like hell with no way out. Even if they are fortunate enough to get a well-paying job after university, they quickly realize a salary cannot lead to financial freedom. Sure, we hear of people making it big in today's society, but for the most part, the majority of our population is still struggling financially. As the cost of living increases and the marketplace shifts, thinking of the future can be very daunting. Unless you figure out a way (as Kris did) to create your own economy.

How did Kris go from struggle and no hope of financial prosperity to his dream lifestyle?

Simple. Kris found a way to turn himself into an investor in the Real Estate industry. He learned how to make money in his own way independent of a boss or a bank. After being a full-time Real Estate investor for the past four years, Kris is reaping the lavish benefits of his hard work in both active and passive income. When he started out, he had no money, poor credit scores, and no experience.

Perhaps very similar to where you might be now. By simply adhering to certain fundamental principles, the same ones you'll be learning in this book, and doing things in a certain way, he's now able to lead an affluent lifestyle. Kris knew life would never be the same again when one of his deals brought in 65,000 in profit and he experienced that first-time thrill of making more money in a few months than he'd ever made his entire life. From that point on, he went all in and has been reaping the benefits ever since. The same thing could happen for you if you only take this book and implement the secrets contained within.

What to expect from this book:

Real estate investing has always been considered a game for more prominent players in society. Those with cash and status often make it work for them. Andrew Carnegie said, "ninety percent of all millionaires become so through owning real estate. More money has been made in real estate than in all industrial investments combined. The wise young man or wage earner of today invests his money in real estate."

His words ring true even in this age of the Internet and technology. No one can deny the Internet has made it possible for us to create new income-producing channels, but at the end of the day, Real Estate is always going to be a no-brainer.

As long as human beings are civilized and living in houses, there will always be plenty of money to be made. Now let me ask you this: Would you like to dip your toes into this lucrative industry and make money your own way?

Will you choose to take the wise words of Carnegie and become a man or woman who invests in Real Estates and makes millions?

If you answered yes, then this book will help you map out the journey of being a smart Real Estate Investor.

It doesn't matter how much experience or cash you have. Once you've made the decision that you must make this happen for you, implementing the strategies and tactics shared in this book will naturally yield results for you.

This book will teach you the fundamentals of Real Estate investing and how to make it the vehicle that helps you retire early and lead a wealthy lifestyle. As I said, you don't even need to have prior experience.

If you're a total beginner with little to no cash as well, this is unquestionably for you.

If you've always dreamed of becoming a millionaire in this lifetime, before you're too old to enjoy life, then this book is definitely for you. It will break down simple ways of starting out, how to find incredible deals, how to analyze those deals, finance them and create profitable exit strategies.

The education you need if you want financial freedom:

Although people like to make real estate elusive and confusing, I can assure you, it's not rocket science. Any man or woman can create significant success in real estate investing with proper planning and execution. Before that can become a reality for you, however, you need to recognize the importance of getting the right education. Your education becomes the first step up the ladder of real estate success.

Without the right education, your ability to navigate the real estate market becomes mitigated and constricted. Whether you're a novice or a seasoned real estate investor education will always play an integral part in your business success. Statistics show that many people involved in real estate fail to achieve financial independence throughout their investment career (even though this is one of the safest forms of investments), not because they lack money but because they lack the right knowledge to do the right thing.

To succeed as a real estate investor you must be resourceful no doubt, but you also need the right knowledge. You must acquire the information that can help you become a better investor. Information that will enable you to know which choice is right for you and your clients.

As our digital economy morphs the real estate industry, it is becoming more than just "land investments." It's now expanded into an information exchange as well. Your customer holds the primary power, and they have access to the Internet. At any given point, these clients are using the Internet to acquire information. In fact, by the end of 2015, it was found that ninety-two percent of clients are doing web searches for shopping for a home and forty-two percent of clients believe that virtual tours do play a decisive role in purchasing a property.

People are finding their dream home through online searches now, and by the time you encounter a buyer, unless they live in a cave with no cellphone and Wi-Fi coverage, they've probably Goggled their problem first. Which means the best way for you to secure a deal is to be as informed as possible about your market. Information and a good strategy are critical. Your clients will trust you more when they find that you are an honest, trustworthy, knowledgeable and resourceful person. So before you downplay the importance of diligently going through this book or the importance of taking an excellent online course on real estate, do some homework on the current state of the marketplace and what it takes to succeed in today's digitally connected world. Money alone will not bring you the success and financial freedom you desire as a real estate investor.

How to use this book:

Unfortunately, the world of Real Estate investing is often overwhelming and confusing for the average person. Without proper education, it's likely you'll burn out and burn through your cash quicker than a gambling addict in Las Vegas. The purpose of this book is to help you avoid the common pitfalls of Real Estate investing. It outlines for you the fundamentals, so you can finally get ahead in life.

No longer will you need to feel as if you have to risk everything with your investments. Instead, I'll walk you through every strategy to find the right one that's right for you and the quality of life you wish to have. The best way to get the most out of this book is to take it a chapter at a time and implement on each section of the roadmap provided. Don't treat this as entertainment or motivation. Make things practical for yourself. Commit to taking action with every gained lesson, and you will come out a winner in this economy.

Whether you want to get started with Rental Properties, flipping houses, house hacking, student rentals or Wholesaling I've got you covered.

Some of what you'll learn includes:

• Why Real Estate is the key to early retirement and financial freedom.

• What the wealthiest men in the world know about Real Estate that you don't.

• The basics you need to know to make Real Estate work for you.

• How to minimize your risk as you start doing Real Estate deals.

• The difference between traditional Real Estate and the new innovative ways that people are leveraging today.

• The best Niches and strategies that you can dive into even as a beginner.

• The financial side of Real Estate and how to stay on top of the game.

•The secret to buying properties without any money.

And that's not all.

By the time you're done reading this book, not only will you know the math needed to succeed in this game, but you'll also have the confidence to go search for your next deal. So whether you've dabbled in this before or not, I encourage you to trust in this process and go through each chapter with an open mind ready to implement what you learn.

Let's get started.

Chapter 02: Why Real Estate Is The Key To Early Retirement And Financial Freedom

Is the idea of early retirement appealing to you?

And by early retirement, I don't just mean spending the rest of your days lazily chilling on the beach sipping piña coladas (although you can do that too if that's your dream). Instead what I mean is being in a position to work on projects you love at your own schedule, eliminating the need for a 9-to-5 and spending more time with the people you love. For most people, the dream is to be able to work a few hours a week and still make a great living.

If that's your dream, if you've always wanted to find financial freedom and a stable, safe source of income real estate investing is the perfect tool to get you there.

Think of this book like a beginners crash course meant to help you fast track the learning curve, offer insights on pitfalls to be aware of and provide guidance on best practices. With that comes the need to know which path of real estate investing is going to be lucrative. After all, who wants to put in all the effort, energy, and resources needed if there isn't enough of a reward to balance things out? Well, I can assure you, an abundant harvest awaits you if you choose to plant the right seeds at the right time and tend to them as any good farmer in the field.

Some of the benefits of investing in real estate versus stock or bonds:

At the core of any investment is the income that can be generated. Real estate guarantees a healthy income stream for you if you know what you're doing. It's a dependable monthly income that you can rely on regardless of economic fluctuations.

Even if you own rentals that aren't doing so well, chances are you'll be making more reliable income than someone who has invested in other assets like stocks or bonds. That doesn't mean stock investment is a bad idea, it just means if you want something safe that is sure to appreciate over time, and if you don't like drama and the suspense of market flops, then real estate is the better option. If you invest in a low-cost index fund of the entire stock market, you're probably going to create enormous wealth in the long run, but when first starting out, real estate is more advantageous in comparison to other passive investments.

For early retirees, it matters even more because real estate investing gets you steady income immediately whereas much of the game in stocks and bonds requires you never to touch it.

Real estate gives you more control over your money, how quickly you grow and the deals you invest in. Your skills and hustle become your best assets when you get into Real Estate investing. And if like so many people you lack cash for funding, your people skills become even more valuable. With a real estate deal, you can significantly improve a property and increase its rent and perceived value. And when you're also the one managing the properties well on the backend, that income stream remains under your control for years to come.

Take the example of an index fund again. Can you really control it?

Not quite. You can control when to buy, reinvent your dividends and when to sell it. End of story. The managers and employees of the companies you buy have more control over your success and income than you do.

There is no right or wrong in either of these options. But personally, it feels better when I know I can influence and control my investments.

Another added benefit of investing in real estate is timing. Real estate investing gives us something most passive index investments can't. The ability to time my wealth building efforts.

As someone with big dreams of financial freedom and early retirement, I'm guessing you've done your goal setting, and there's a due date you set for yourself. The only way to ensure your investments are growing and helping you reach that goal on time is by investing in the right things that are guaranteed to increase over a specific period. Preferably sooner rather than later.

With investments like stock indexes, growth can be extremely volatile over the short run. You always feel at the mercy of the stock prices, and if there should ever be a sudden dip or drop in stock prices, you can kiss your due date goodbye. No chance of financial independence if the stock prices act up. This has been experienced a lot recently with Bitcoin and crypto-currency. It's a great game but a highly volatile one that's better suited for people who enjoy the drama and thrill of being in a never-ending roller coaster.

With real estate investing, however, you can breathe with ease because none of that drama and volatility applies. You have two very predictable growth options:

1. Positive rental income
2. Debt amortization (pay down)

Reliable rental income:

Although I'm not here to make ridiculous claims that cannot be backed up (and we all know any type of investments does require risk management), as a general rule, real estate has shown it can remain quite stable even during the worst times.

Take for example the housing crisis that hit some years ago. On the surface, it appeared as though things were going really bad, right? However, research issued by the U.S Census Bureau on January 30, 2018, surveying current population and housing vacancy during the recession years as well as before that shows that even at the worst times in the market (2008-2010), rents still remained stable or only experienced a slight decrease in most U.S markets. Of course, everything else including housing prices themselves plummeted.

All this to state that although one is never wholly guaranteed that the investment will be completely secure in future as things change, suffice it so say investing in this industry is as close as you can get to a guaranteed win.

Amortization:

Ever heard of a debt snowball? With a debt snowball plan, you can apply extra savings to pay off your mortgages faster than initially planned. Say twenty years earlier. In so doing, you reduce the risk involved and increase your income just in time to match that due date of early retirement.

These are predictable ways of determining when and how your wealth grows, and for the most part, you can easily control them. There are various types of real estate investments that help make these ideas practical, and in the next chapter, we get to dive deep into all the best types of real estate you can invest in. Some of these you've probably heard of before or even dabbled in and some might be new, either way, you'll get to know only the best of the best that we know work.

Before we jump into the next chapter, however, let's clarify some misconceptions and myths that have caused a lot of impediment for aspiring or newbie real estate investors.

Myths about real estate investing revealed:

I must admit, some of these myths (okay most of them) really crippled me when I first started out. There were many occasions where I passed on an opportunity because I was still under the false belief of some of these myths and it took me far too long to break free. If only I had known ten years ago what I know today, my real estate journey would have been less nightmarish.

To save you from the pitfalls I kept falling into, here are some myths you need to debunk before becoming a successful real estate investor. Do a self-check as you go through each and see if any of them resonate as that will show you which areas need some work.

Myth #1: Real estate is only for the wealthy.

Actually, it's not just for the wealthy. It's for anyone who is willing to do what the masses won't.

So many people think they need to have money in the bank, high credit scores or connections to succeed in real estate investing. It couldn't be further away from the truth.

The truth is, it doesn't matter how much money you do or don't have right now. It doesn't even matter whether you own credit cards or how bad your credit scores are. You don't need to have any assets whatsoever, to get started in real estate.

Depending on your current situation, you could start as a wholesaler as I did, or you could flip houses. You could also jump in headfirst and start doing rental properties.

As long as you've set your goals right and you have a reliable road map, even without money in the bank, good credit scores or a job, you can still make real estate work.

How?

You must learn the skills needed to be a good salesperson, and marketer. You also need the right skills to speak with investors and get their attention. Leveraging your sweat equity, time and knowledge can be a precious thing when done strategically. The better you get at helping investors see tremendous opportunity in working with you, the quicker you can turn your idea into a profit machine.

One of my real estate friends and mentor told me that when he started two decades ago, he didn't think it would even be possible for him to own 26 units within two years of getting started. That was the impossible goal that he set for himself. It took him eighteen months to crush it and reach his goal. I have countless stories of people who've been able to start from nothing (including myself) and build something meaningful.

Myth busting:

Real estate investing isn't just for the wealthy in society. Anyone can get started in it using different strategies to create income streams that turn the small idea into an empire. The top 1% of the wealthy on the planet all share this commonality. They all participate in real estate investing, and some started with nothing and built great careers and businesses thanks to real estate.

Myth #2: Making money with real estate is quick and easy

This myth is fueled by the "get rich quick" mentality, which never ends well. If you're looking for shortcuts in life and lazy ways to make money where you don't add any value or put in the effort for the rewards desired, then I recommend staying away from real estate.

I know that's not what marketers will tell you. Everyone will attempt to get you to buy into his or her program or product by over exaggerating the truth.

The truth is, like any worthwhile endeavor, real estate investing requires patience, perseverance, and persistence. Believing false stories around real estate riches is setting yourself up for failure. The more knowledge you have, the better you get at execution and implementation, the higher your chances of success in the business.

Myth busting:

Making money in real estate isn't a matter of luck, there are no shortcuts, and it's not a get rich quick scheme. You need to put in the work to reap the rewards. Determination, patience and a success mindset are a must-have. When starting out, you must be willing to invest a considerable portion of your time and effort to produce profit, especially with rental properties.

Myth#3: I need to own my own home before I can be a real estate investor.

No, you don't.

Picture this for a moment. You successfully invest in your first single family home. After which, you rent it out for $3,000 per month. Meanwhile, you're staying in a house that costs you $1,000 per month, and you pay $1,000 as the mortgage for the property you invested in. See where I'm going with this?

Investing in real estate could be an excellent way for you to finance property and have it pay for itself and for your cost of living as well. Simple right?

Myth busting:

You don't need to own a home to become a real state investor. But you do need the right strategy and a little creativity.

Myth #4: I need to form a real estate limited liability company (LLC) first before I can make my first deal.

Actually, unless you are rich and famous and buying large properties of five units and above or commercial real estate, then the simple answer is - this is just a myth. You don't need to form an LLC.

From a practical standpoint, most people starting out have minimal assets to protect. Many people have little to negative net worth. And even if you have a few rental properties, chances are the bank owns 80% of the property, so you don't really own it. No one can take something you don't own. So for the majority of new investors, an LLC should not be a priority.

Myth busting:

You don't need an LLC. I'm not saying you should never get one! What I am saying is that for practical reasons, it can wait until you actually grow a thriving business. Consider the fact that there are expenses associated with maintaining an LLC and most of the time; the perceived protection that an LLC offers can be easily pierced especially if you are an owner-manager. If you have considerable assets then yes, by all means, have legal entities protecting you. If you are a high-profile wealthy person, I also advocate getting one as soon as possible. But if you're just starting out, trying to hustle to make your first deal happen, you probably don't need an LLC.

Myth #5: I need a lot of experience to be a real estate investor.

It is true that experience makes us better at our craft regardless of industry, but it is not true that you need to have the experience to get started.

Experience is a matter of practice. So if you're just starting out, why would you allow yourself to get hindered by the fact that you don't yet have experience?

Can you remember the first time you rode a bike or drove a car? Did you have experience?

Of course not. It took hands-on practice to learn these skills. The more you did it, the better you became until you attained mastery. The same is true with any type of investing especially real estate.

Myth busting:

It's okay that you have no experience when starting out. That comes over time. Learn as many strategies as you can, implement and experiment to find what works best for you.

Start with basic skills, keep learning and improving. Build upon each skill as you scale to the next level and before you know it, you'll achieve all your goals.

Myth #6: Banks are the only way to finance my real estate deals

This is an easy one for many of us to believe. I totally fell for it too because I didn't think there was any other way for me to get money aside from a job or a bank. But I was wrong...

And I have proved it time and time again that this myth is total BS.

Now, don't be too hard on yourself if you're still stuck in this belief. It just takes a shift in perspective and learning from those who've found other alternatives for financing. In an upcoming chapter, I'm spilling all I've learned so you can be free from this myth as well.

Myth busting:

Although this is usually the common route people take, banks aren't the only way to fund your deals. And if your credit score is as bad as mine used to be when I first got started, no bank will even consider loaning you any money.

Besides, banks cap you out anyways because they have so many restrictive rules and regulations even if your credit scores aren't too bad. Private investors are an excellent alternative and my number one recommendation. All you need to learn is the skill of raising private capital from individuals who are grateful that you can skillfully use their cash and credit in a way that brings them a profit (whatever their idea of profit is). If you can learn to create win-win scenarios and communicate this effectively to private investors, you can quickly and easily grow your real estate business.

Myth #7: Real estate is guaranteed to bring me passive income

Not exactly!

I'm sure you've heard over and over again this idea that real estate investing is a passive investment. There is some truth to it, but you're not being shown the full picture. So let me shed some light here. If you jump in blindly thinking this will immediately become a passive income (and you don't have to lift a finger ever again), you might end up severely depressed when that doesn't pan out.

Certain investing strategies are classified as passive income for the investor, but even these don't just happen magically overnight.

Imagine if you will - investing in a multifamily home where you have long term monthly rent. This is technically speaking a form of passive income, but I can assure you, there's a lot of effort, time, resources and money that goes into the acquiring of this property and the tenants. And although once you have the tenants long-term, you don't need to do very much, as the property investor you'll still need to be involved in maintaining the property.

Myth busting:
Passive income in real estate investing is possible, but even then, the strategy will require some sort of involvement.

Myth #8: I should only invest in real estate that's in my local neighborhood

Many real estate gurus will say that one should just buy property that's within 30minutes driving distance from where they live. This isn't always the best solution for everyone. It indeed wasn't right for me, so you need to figure out what your goals are and then work out a strategy and choose the niche that helps you achieve those goals.

Suppose your goal is to replace your income, retire early and eventually gain full financial freedom but you live in an area where real estate is costly. Unfortunately, your local neighborhood may not be the right place to start because it's highly unlikely that you'll find properties that produce immediate positive cash flow. This concept of just buying where you live is a one size fits all approach, and we all know real estate investing doesn't have a one size fits all solution.

Myth busting:

There is no need for you to feel stuck with your real estate investing if where you live doesn't seem to match the criterion needed to help you reach your objectives. Simply get resourceful and creative, do your research well and find areas that have a low crime rate, where the population is increasing and the price to rent ratio is closer to the 1% rule. In chapter six where we break down the most popular and most profitable real estate strategies, you'll see how to invest in a property that generates passive income while being far away from you.

Understanding the fundamentals

Good real estate investors do not strive to get rich quick. They are not interested in overnight success. Thriving real estate investors enter the game fully informed and aware of the dedication, perseverance, and hard work and self-learning they'll need to take on, and they are willing to go all in.

Are you?

If your answer is absolutely yes - then it's time to step up.

The game is about to begin, and we need to be fully prepped for what is ahead. That means, understanding the basics. There are certain real estate concepts you need to know before jumping head first into the world of real estate investing. Failure to understand these concepts means you will encounter more overwhelm, confusion and roadblocks than is necessary.

Ever been to a doctor's office to get treatment only to come out feeling a bit confused because nothing he said made sense, but you paid a hefty fee anyway and trusted that he knows what he's doing?

It happens to me a lot. Sometimes I come out with a list of medication, take them to the pharmacy and trust that between the words on the paper and the knowledge of the pharmacist, I will receive the right medication prescribed to me which by the way I can't even pronounce. There's a lot of blind faith involved in such situations (for many of us).

Real estate investing should not be like that for you. If you don't speak and understand the "real estate language" you won't go very far. It is your job to self educate and master the language.

Let's start with a basic real estate dictionary to help you out. A more comprehensive glossary can be found at the end of this book.

Basic Beginner's glossary:

1. Appreciation

Appreciation refers to the increase in the value of a property over time. There are many reasons why a property appreciates over time. Sometimes it can be a result of inflation, an increase in demand or a decrease in the supply of properties. It can also be due to added value as a result of property improvements such as adding a pool, upgrading the kitchen or adding an extra room.

Appreciation is usually projected as a percentage of the property's value over the course of a year.

2. Cash Flow

This is the flow of money in and out of business. In the real estate business, it is the rent generated by the monthly rent collected minus all the monthly expenses such as mortgages, taxes, HOA fees, etc. When investing in real estate, always look for positive cash flow from the property.

Gross rent - Expenses = Cash flow

3. Cash Flow Property

This is an investment property that generates a surplus of money each month after all expenses have been paid. Cash flow properties are highly sought after, and they should be your primary target as a real estate investor.

4. Commercial Real Estate

This is defined in contrast to residential real estate and encompasses industrial properties, medical facilities, retail centers, office buildings, and multifamily complexes. Commercial real estate can also be used to refer to land that will be developed into a commercial project in the future.

5. Capitalization Rate (Cap Rate)

This is the rate of return on your investment property based on the income the property is expected to generate. It is used to determine the value of a real estate investment. The Cap rate percentage is found by dividing the net operating income of a real estate asset (expenses minus income) by the current value of the asset. The Cap rate is always calculated using the current value of the asset, rather than the purchased value of the asset.

A simple formula to use is:

Cap Rate = Net Operating Income/Market Value

6. Cash on Cash Return (CoC)

This is the annual return/income an investor receives in relation to the down payment. It refers to the annual cash return of a property divided by the amount of cash invested. If a property is purchased outright with no leverage, this can also be referred to as the property's cap rate. In the case where a property is purchased using leverage, this number differs from the property's overall return, as it does not include the equity gained by the principal portion of the mortgage payment.

A simple formula to use is:

Cash on Cash Return = Net Operating Income/Total Cash Investment

7. Debt Coverage Ratio (DCR)

This is the ratio that expresses the number of times annual net operating income exceeds debt, i.e., total loan payment. A simple formula to use is:

Debt Coverage Ratio = Net Operating income/Debt

- Less than 1.0 - not enough NOI to cover the debt

- Exactly 1.0 - just enough NOI to cover the debt

- Greater than 1.0 - more than enough NOI to cover the debt

8. Equity

This is the difference between the current market value of a property and the amount owed by the owner on a mortgage (if any).

It is essentially how much stake in ownership on a piece of property is worth. If there is mortgage involved then as it gets paid off, the owner's equity grows.

When a property is being sold, the equity is the difference between the purchase price and the sale price. Usually, the market drives the property's equity; however, if a property is improved or upgraded, the equity value can increase.

9. Gross Scheduled Income (GSI)

This is the annual rental income an investment property would generate if all units were rented and the rent was collected in full. In the case where there are vacancies, count that in your calculation at their market rent. A simple formula to use is:

Gross scheduled income = Rental Income + Vacant units

10. Gross Operating Income (GOI)

This is the amount of income needed (that you'll collect) to service the rental property. A simple formula to use is:

Gross operating income = Gross scheduled income - Vacancy and Credit Loss + other income

11. Internal Rate of Return (IRR)

This is the point at which the net value of investment expenses equals the net value of assets income. These are both calculated at the current value of the investment and not the purchased or future value of the property. It helps establish the growth potential of an investment. The IRR can be used to indicate the point at which an investment could become profitable. If an internal rate of return is above a pre-defined number, it is an acceptable investment.

12. Individual Retirement Account Investing (IRA investing)

This refers to using your IRA or retirement account to invest in property. Returns on property purchased with an IRA are generally tax-deferred. However, profits must go back into the IRA account and cannot be spent before retirement. IRA investing allows people to transfer funds to a self-directed IRA to purchase real estate. It's also possible to use it the funds in an IRA account to obtain a mortgage or any other type of investment property.

13. Leverage Return

This is the return calculated on an investment that takes advantage of a mortgage. It should not be confused with cash on cash return. Leverage return includes the principal pay down as part of the return. Although using leverage return is slightly riskier, it is advantageous to the investor as it provides higher yields and enables the investor to diversify across multiple properties.

It is calculated by subtracting the expenses incurred by the property (including the interest payment on the mortgage) from the income produced by the property and dividing that by the initial investment amount. A simple formula to use is:

Leverage Return = Income - Expenses (including interest payment) / Initial Investment amount

14. Leasing Fee

This is a fee paid to the property manager when they sign a lease with a new tenant. If the tenant renews their contract, there is a re-leasing fee.

15. Net Operating Income (NOI)

This is the rental property's income after discounting all expenses. A simple formula to use is:

Net Operating Income = Gross Operating Income - Operating Expenses

16. Operating Expenses

This is the cost of running the investment property. That includes property taxes, insurance, utilities, and all maintenance costs. That does not cover any payments made for mortgages, capital expenditures or income taxes.

17. Operating Expense Ratio (OER)

This is the ratio between the total operating expenses to gross operating income, which is always expressed as a percentage. A simple formula to use is:

OER = (Operating Expenses/Gross Operating Income) X 100

18. Retail Investor

A retail investor is also known as an individual investor or a small investor. These types of investors buy and sell investment asses for their personal account building their own portfolios. They are defined as such in contrast to institutional investors. As a general rule, small investors invest lower amounts than institutional investors.

19. Real Estate Owned (REO)

This refers to a property that is owned by a lender, usually a bank. Lenders generally only take the title of properties after an unsuccessful selling attempt at a foreclosure auction. REO properties are often excellent for purchasing below market value, which makes them highly sought after by investors.

20. Remote Investing

This type of investing refers to the ability to be able to invest in and own property that is geographically removed from your primary residence. In traditional real estate, the prevailing trend was for real estate investors to purchase property that is "in their backyard." This was chiefly because it made it easier to manage and monitor the investment. It often meant the investor would also be the landlord and needed to keep up with daily maintenance and running of the property.

Remote investors, however, do not follow this old trend. They purchase property in areas that have favorable returns. Remote investing allows investors to take advantage of lower property costs or higher rents that may not be available near their primary residence.

21. Rehabilitation

This refers to the repairs that need to be done to make an asset tenant-ready. Primary inspection is imperative before making any purchase to ensure extensive renovations aren't necessary. Rehabilitation can include minor fixes such as paint and lighting upgrades, but they can also extend to substantial repairs such as roof replacement and plumbing upgrades.

In the event of a large-scale rehabilitation, the investor should be notified before the purchase. Costs associated with improvement are generally included in the purchase price.

22. 1% Rule

This is the rent to expense ratio that an investment property must have to be profitable. There are many variables and expenses to take into account but in general, for an investment property to have a positive ROI the rent on that property must be at least 1% of the purchase price. This is considered a favorable investment asset in the real estate world.

23. Single Family Rentals (SFRs)

This refers to a freestanding residential property designed to house one family. It is purchased by an investor and rented to a tenant. SFRs are defined as such in contrast to multi-family property, though properties up to a fourplex are sometimes classified as SFRs as well. Properties with more than four units are called multi-family properties. Families are generally very interested in single-family properties. From an investment perspective, we may consider them steadier as families (especially with children) tend to stay in one place longer.

24. Self Directed IRA (SDIRA)

A self-directed individual retirement account is a type of account that provides tax benefits to money deposited for retirement. Any income from the account is taxed at the tax bracket the account holder reaches upon retirement, which is often much lower than their pre-retirement tax bracket. There is a significant difference between a regular IRA account and a self-directed IRA (SDIRA) account in that the permitted investments aren't identical.

In addition to traditional stocks and bonds, a SDIRA account can be used to invest in alternative investments such as tax liens, notes, and real estate. The money in the SDIRA account can be invested just as the funds in any standard account as long as the dividends are returned to the account. Funds cannot be accessed until the account holder reaches retirement, however. And all asset expenses must be paid for using funds from the account.

A SDIRA can also be used to hold a mortgage although this loan (non-recourse loan), different from regular mortgages is often at a higher rate. It does, however, allow investors to leverage their funds to create a higher ROI.

25. Turn Key Property (TKP)

A TKP is a property that has been purchased, rehabbed and rented to a tenant and is now back in the market for sale to another investor. These types of properties usually provide cash flow from the moment the investor purchases it since the property is already rented.

26. Vacancy Provision

This refers to the money that investors set aside to prepare for a future vacancy. It is a percentage of the monthly rent. The average vacancy provision is 6% for vacancy and 6% for maintenance

You will find a more in-depth list of all the real estate investing terms in the last chapter of this book. For now, you're well equipped to move to the next level of this journey where we discuss the different types of real estate and which ones will be best for you.

Before wrapping up this chapter, there's one more thing I need to mention.

The one size fits all model doesn't work.

It's a broken concept and if you find anyone attempting to teach to you, turn and run really fast.

You are a unique individual with unique skills, goals, motives, and aptitudes. The right model that works to earn me millions may not be the best one to lead you to your millions. We can exchange ideas and insights, and I can even share with you how I search for, evaluate, negotiate and sell my deals for a profit (which

I will in this book), but that does not guarantee you will have the same success copying me. It is therefore imperative you become your own influencer.

You must become your chief guru and learn to trust in your gut, your skills, and your ability to make this work. The real estate investment is meant to be the vehicle; you are the driver and the determining factor. If your head is in the game and you've customized your blueprint for real estate success, whichever model you choose will work. Having that right mindset, confidence and trust in yourself are priceless and perhaps the secret ingredient that will take you that extra mile. If you're ready to go all the way, I'm here to guide you into the next phase of this beginners crash course.

Chapter 03: What Are The Risks Involved In Real Estate?

Like any other form of investment, real estate carries with it significant risks. I don't think the risks are higher than investments such as stock market trading and crypto technologies. But since you don't want to go into the real estate investing business blindly, let's make sure you understand the risks at hand. After all, everyone would be a successful millionaire if real estate investing had zero risks involved.

One of the most significant risks in real estate investing is landing on a deal or many deals that turn into negative cash flows. If you find yourself at the end of a deal with less money than you started with, you'll be stuck in what's known as negative cash flow. The issue with a negative cash flow is you'll quickly go broke.

Cash is king in real estate. And you need positive cash flow.

If you don't get good at generating cash flow with your deals, it's going to be tough reaching your financial goals or retiring early. Make sure you learn how to find and analyze real estate investments so you can spot the good from the bad ones. And trust me, there will be plenty of bad deals that look "okay" on the surface.

There's also an environmental risk to take to account. Imagine buying or building a property in an area that was under jurisdiction. Surely that would spell doom for your return on investment. I witnessed such a scenario with an acquaintance some years back. The raw land he bought and constructed apartment complexes hadn't been well vetted. Turns out it was under government jurisdiction, and they ended up in a very long and draining dispute. Do your due diligence well and be smart with the choices you make especially at the start where every penny counts.

Speaking about money, let's talk about the risk involved in getting too much debt for investing. Do you know debt magnifies the investment risk?

The more debt you have, the riskier that investment. And since interest rates are never constant, you can struggle a lot with increased or fluctuating financial costs, which is undoubtedly not good for you. Minimize this type of risk as much as possible.

Another potential risk that could lead to loss is getting stuck with a deal that has no profitable exit strategy. If a deal goes south, and you've already invested in it, how quickly can you exit that deal and will it still profit you?

You must always have a logical, doable, clear and specific exit strategy before getting into a deal. There has to be a contingency plan in place to pull you out of the weeds in case you need it. Whether you intend to do a fix and flip right away or to lease and hold it for 10 years, always have a good exit strategy to mitigate the risk.

There will always be risk involved, but with continued education, proper planning, and some experience you'll be able to do effective risk management as your business grows.

Before going after your first deal, get this right:

The only way to financial freedom, early retirement, and steady passive income is by changing your mindset. Without the right mindset, it doesn't matter how many books you read or which guru you learn from. All of it will be in vain.

Whatever is taking place between your ears determines how successful you become in real estate and in life. You need an abundance mindset, and you need to be right mentally if you want to be a thriving real estate investor. Here's what I mean by this.

On the one hand, you need to have an abundance mindset that recognizes opportunity and trusts in the fact that there will always be someone ready and motivated to sell his or her property. Someone with a problem to which you can provide a solution quickly, effectively and professionally.

On the other hand, being right mentally means you can't just approach this business haphazardly. Whether you're doing it full-time or as a side hustle, you still need to give it the deserved attention and serve your clients diligently and with excellence. You need to be committed, not just interested in succeeding.

Having interest is not the same as being committed. For example, a woman who desires to shed some weight may buy a workout program out of interest. She might even start doing runs around the park once or twice a week because she's interested in getting back in shape. If it rains on that particular day when she ought to be out running, she'll probably skip it and wait till the weather is better. If she has a long week at work, she'll probably skip her DVD workout program for that week and chose to focus on work instead. That's having an interest in training.

Another woman, however, is a professional marathon runner. Whether it rains or shines, she's going to be doing her workout relentlessly. If running in the park is part of her daily routine, she's going to be out there even in the snow. That's being committed to training.

Going to seminars, watching real estate investors on YouTube, reading books and magazines is great and highly entertaining. It can also be very motivating especially if you're being entertained by a high power presenter. But this won't get you results. It will satisfy your interest but not your bank account. Even reading this book can pass as a form of entertainment. So you need to do a gut check because if satisfying your interest is more dominant than the commitment of taking consistent action on the things you learn, real estate will not make you a millionaire. Having an abundance mindset and being mentally committed and in the game of winning is critical. Ultimately, only you know where you currently stand and the results you'll have at the end of this year will be a perfect reflection of that.

How to deal with bad credit scores

Can you really become a real estate investor if you have a bad credit score and too much debt?

There's no simple answer to this. Why?

Because in truth, you can still become a real estate investor. However, it may not be a good idea to start investing just yet. Here's why.

Have you ever taken the time to think about what the credit score even means?

Your credit score is merely a number that represents your financial ability to manage your money. And before you come to the conclusion that I'm just trying to be a jerk, know that I am sharing this advice with your and ME.

We could all get better at managing our money. We could all use more education on debt, taxes and how to improve credit scores. And even though you don't actually need credit to invest in real estate, I think it's important to get real with yourself and recognize where you have money habits that aren't serving you.

If you do have money habits that are detrimental to you, no amount of real estate investing will help you. That's a problem you need to resolve first.

For most people, poor credit scores are a result of reckless spending. Buying things you don't really need to please people who don't even care about your well-being. Sometimes it could be a result of an addiction. Other times it could be the painful student loans, medical bills, unemployment or other distressing situations where one feels lost for options. Regardless of your reasons for a poor credit score, you must make sure you've resolved the problem at the core.

So tell me, what does your written budget look like? Do you even have a written budget?

When was the last time you read a book on credit repair? When was the last time you used your credit card to buy something because you couldn't afford it otherwise? Food is an exception.

If you answer these questions right here and now truthfully, you'll begin to see the relationship you have with credit and how well you're managing your money.

If you're not good at managing credit, you won't be good at handling what real estate investors call "good debt." And even though there are ways to invest without credit (or with poor credit scores), unless you've cured yourself of the disease of credit drama, you'll keep falling into the pit of despair because real estate will never solve your money drama.

Let's touch on ways you can start improving your credit score.

Start educating yourself on how to repair your credit scores. Even though you don't need it now, as your business grows, you will want that option of being able to get a sweet deal from the bank. Remember Kris from earlier? He now wants to invest in a 60-unit apartment, and one of his options is leveraging the great credit he's built up over time.

One of my students started off with less than 300 and has over time built up his credit score to mid 700. He is currently working on the 60-unit apartment building with Kris. The only way this is possible for him is due to the fact that even as a beginner, he's coming in with great leverage that someone like Kris who has more experience in the game is very interested in.

There are countless resources online that can help you slowly improve your credit card, and if though you can still implement what's on this book without credit or with poor credit scores, I cannot urge you enough to work on making it better. Your future investor self will thank you for the work you put it no when it's time to buy your million dollar property.

Let's talk about debt.

Is debt good for you?

Depends on whether you have good debt or bad debt. Trust me, there is a huge difference. The average hard working person can't tell the difference though. He or she generally uses debt to acquire liabilities instead of assets. This is part of the reason financial freedom is so elusive to the masses. They keep buying things that generally lose value over time, and it soon becomes an addiction, which takes years to get out of.

If you want the debt to work for you, you'll need to increase your financial intelligence. You need to learn how to use debt to grow your worth and how to invest in assets that produce cash flow.

Good debt brings you income. It's debt that is used to acquire an investment such as a property, which brings you income and pays for the debt itself. Bad debt just takes money out of your pocket. Credit card debt is a great example.

Did you know that almost half of the US households have some kind of credit card debt? The average amount of this credit card debt is about $10,000. That's crazy!

But what's more alarming is that because there's a deficiency of right financial education, even the people who somehow manage to get out of bad debt soon find themselves in it.

Unless you start doing something significantly different and increase your financial intelligence, early retirement will pass you by. It's good to know where you stand in relation to debt. Credit card debt is one of the easiest traps to fall into. Applying for a new card takes little and swiping away your card has little immediate consequences, but at the end of the month, things start to get a bit scary once you see those interest rates increasing money owed.

How much bad debt do you currently have?

Do you have a plan to eliminate that debt and start building up good debt that helps you get richer? The sooner you can free yourself from bad debt, the quicker you'll achieve financial freedom.

When it comes to using good debt to generate wealth, you first need to shift your perception of debt. Society has primed us to believe any kind of debt is terrible. This is just not true. Good debt (if you know what you're doing) can be very good for you. Imagine getting a loan to buy a property that you rent out for

$3000. If your monthly debt is $1000, you'll have a cash flow investment that pays its own debt and puts money in your pocket to cover all your other expenses.

How to invest with poor credit scores and create good debt

As I said before, the good news is you can still become a successful real estate investor even if you dealing with bad debt and poor credit scores. Here are some suggestions that may work for you. I dive deep into many of them in upcoming chapters when we talk more about financing, but I want you to start seeing that as long as you have the hustle, there will always be a way for you to create success in real estate investing.

•Get a hard money lender

Hard money lenders are usually not interested in your credit scores because they care more about the security in the deal. They want to know that no matter what, they'll make money. Many hard money lenders were once investors, so they know the game, and as long as you've done your job securing a great deal, this can be an excellent way to make your money. Remember though, they usually give you under two years to pay back the loan and charge high-interest rates.

•Private money lenders

These are individuals (some you might even know personally) who want to achieve a good return on their investments. They are typically not real estate investors or professionals, and all they want is to know their money is with someone they can trust and that it will yield a profit.

•Seller financing

If you can be smart enough to get seller financing, it can be a powerful way to grow your real estate business without any outside help. It offers a great win-win scenario for all parties, and most sellers have no interest in your credit scores.

•Partnerships

This is a favorite for many others and me. It's about forging alliances with people who complete you but have the same objective.

There's something you have that I lack and vice versa. By partnering up, we fill that void, power things up and create favorable outcomes. Perhaps you have bad credit, but maybe you have something I don't such as time, sales skills, hustle, etc. By bringing something valuable and unique to the table, you make it possible for both of us to achieve our goals simultaneously.

Be sure to vet your partner thoroughly and be careful to choose someone with shared values.

• Wholesaling

For those with poor credit, this is perhaps the most talked about method. Every guru is promoting wholesaling and with good reason. If you know what you're doing, you can run an entire deal without using a single dollar of your own money or ever needing your credit checked. But I must warn you - this is hard. It is a job, and you need to be really patient, committed, and because there are legal implications regarding wholesaling, I recommend getting a license first.

Now let's spend some time dissecting the old world of real estate vs. the new world that makes it easier for anyone to become a real estate investor.

Chapter 04: Traditional Real Estate Investing Vs. Innovative Real Estate Investing

Traditional real estate has been the same for the last 100 years or so with very minimum shifts. People usually buy and sell houses using real estate agents as the gatekeeper. In the United States, about ninety percent of transactions involve an agent while the remaining ten percent do private sales. In the U.K agents take up more than ninety percent of the share.

In the old days, this was probably the only business model to follow if you wanted to be part of the real estate game and much of it still continues to take place offline even with the introduction of technology. However, something is starting to shift. The rise of on-demand technology is causing significant changes that are being experienced by the entire industry.

New models are now launching all over the world and investment in the industry is growing. We are now starting to see the emergence of real estate tech companies and innovative entrepreneurs coming out of the woodworks with disruptive concepts that help empower their clients and get the job done.
We are also seeing more creativity in how transactions are carried out.

Perhaps there was a time when you had to be wealthy and have high credit scores to be a real estate investor. That's why people started believing that as the only viable option of entering this business. But as I proved to you in an earlier chapter, this is definitely not the case today. Your possibilities are now endless, and as long as you have the hustle and a good plan, your chances of success are very high with or without capital funding.

Creating your real estate business plan

Creating your business plan is one of the first steps toward long-term success. As any architect will tell you, constructing a beautiful building that lasts over time is impossible without proper planning. This is you ensuring the foundation is solid before breaking ground.

What a business plan is not:

This isn't meant to be rigid rules that constrict you. It's supposed to be a roadmap or a guide that helps you move in the right direction. It gives you a measurable, logical reference point to keep yourself accountable.

With a clearly defined business, you're supposed to feel more motivated, able to envision the end game and carry out the plan from your current starting point.

Here is what your real estate business plan needs to include:

Goals

What objectives matter to you? What would you like to achieve? If you desire to make $10,000 a month from your real estate business, write it down. If your goal is to own 20 units in the next 2 years, write that down. Goals may change over time, and that's okay. As you hit an objective, you'll set a new one and restructure your business. That's how it should be. I recommend setting short-term goals and long-term goals. Make sure these are goals that fire you up and align with your overall vision of your life.

Mission Statement

We've heard from motivational gurus the importance of knowing your "WHY." It's not hype; you do need to know what's driving you to make real estate investing work for you. And it needs to be something deep and meaningful to you so that when things aren't going according to plan (and it always happens), you'll have an anchor to keep you going.

Your mission statement needs to define your purpose, the purpose of your business and how you're going to benefit your clients.

The strategy

As you're about to find out, there are hundreds of ways for you to make money in real estate. That's a good thing. However, you must be careful not to get sidetracked trying to implement all of them at once. In fact, I share the most relevant ones to you in the hopes that you will take just one of these strategies and master it. You don't need to be a master at everything in real estate to make good money. Think of this is choosing a vehicle. You only need one vehicle to move from point A to point B. Your point B is the selected goal. That is your desired destination. Now you simply need to choose the vehicle you'll travel in and stay focused on the journey till you reach the destination. Writing down the strategy of your choice helps to anchor it in. It also gives you the chance to evaluate how well it aligns with your mission, your goals, your current situation and the empire you're building. I've already alluded to the fact that there are many niches and strategies in real estate investing that work regardless of your financial situation. If you're going to work part time or full time on this, you'll also need to pick the appropriate niche and strategy that has the potential of generating the highest return on your investment. Don't worry if you're still unsure which is best for you, come back and fill out this section after going through the next chapter.

Realize also that you can always expand and take advantage of more strategies as you grow and scale the business.

Timeline

Setting smart goals also included giving them an expiration date. You need to pick the desired time that feels realistic but at the same time stretches you. A 23-year-old girl aspiring to be a real estate investor said to me that her goal was to become a millionaire and move to New York by the time she was 25 years old. She gave herself 2 years to go from a complete newbie with no money in the bank, lots of student loans and no mentorship to being a millionaire investor. While it does sound sweet and ambitious, she's setting herself up for failure.

I want you to avoid making yourself the bad guy in the story of your life. Pick a due date for the goals you've just set and do it intelligently knowing that whatever choice you've made, you'll have to be accountable to yourself when the time comes.

The Market

As a beginner, you need to choose an area that you will dominate and the type of properties you'll look for first. You're a new investor with little or no experience so you need to plan on investing in a property that you can easily access. Your local area is often the best and most comfortable place to start because you know the area, feel comfortable enough to live there as well, and it's easy to drive to the property. Of course, there are some exceptions to this in which case you can invest in other areas, but I do recommend starting locally. Identify the local players, start creating allies, learn as much as you can about the properties and opportunities in your local market and you'll find it's easier to become a local superhero. When people trust you, it's easier to do business with you.

Criteria

The next thing we want to make sure you write down in the business plan is a strict criterion of the deals you'll start working on. What kind of deals do you wish to work with? What criterion should each property posses? You also need to define your loan to value, cash flow requirements (critical), the maximum purchase price, the maximum rehabilitation budget, and the maximum timeline. One of my first mentors taught me years ago that having a strict criterion and adhering to it no matter what would save me a lot of heartaches. And he was right.

If a deal doesn't meet your criteria, walk away. Most people won't because they either haven't created a set of rules for themselves or because they get seduced into a deal blindly. Either way, those people usually end up with heart-wrenching stories of deals gone back. I'm not saying you can't land on a bad deal, but at least by having a clearly defined criterion, you can easily recognize properties that won't end up being a good deal, at least ninety-nine percent of the time.

The Marketing Plan

In today's world where people spend most of the time online, it's never been more critical to craft a marketing plan that serves you both offline and online. You can't just depend on traditional marketing methods. According to a study by Facebook, the average person checks his or her phone thirty times a day. However, adults under 40 do it, even more, increasing their range to 150 times a day. And of course, this number is projected to keep growing among all age groups in the coming years. There is great power in technology, and if you're not coming up with creative ways to show up on your clients' mobile phones, you'll not be able to survive and grow in an on-demand environment. So you need to have a marketing plan that helps you reach buyers and sellers effectively. Start thinking of how you can generate constant leads of motivated sellers. Ways for finding the best deals that are listed. Will you use agents, MLS, direct mail to lists, online searches, paid ads or other means?

The Financing

This is usually a very challenging part for many beginners. Today's market requires you get innovative and resourceful especially if you don't have the cash to start with. Write down how you plan to acquire and fund your deals. Will you be using conventional means? Will you get equity partners, seller financing, lease options, hard money lenders or some other innovative method?

There are simple things you can learn to become more attractive to private money lenders which is good because that ensures you always have a steady flow of financing whenever a deal presents itself. We'll cover this more in the chapter on financing your real estate investing.

Your current finances are also essential to include in the business plan. What resources do you have? Are you starting with zero or some equity and cash? Document this and update it as it changes.

Documenting the steps for closing the deals

Carefully write down the steps you are going to use to turn a property purchase into a profit. Include the income and expenses and prepare for the unexpected as well. Detail some of the exit strategies that you know can work in case the plan doesn't go as expected.

Exit strategies

You always need a backup plan for your original plan, and then you need a back up for the backup. I kid you not. Having multiple exit strategies is essential especially in the beginning because without it, you might end up stuck with a property that has no cash flow and that would be hell! So this part should take up a significant portion of your business plan. How are you going to get out of the deal if you need to? Write down as many back up ideas as you've got.

This is where mentorship becomes super useful. Books, seminars, and courses are great, but having a mentor who can share different tricks and perspectives is priceless. That's the stuff you'll never get in a book because it only happens during that live human interaction. A few exist ideas to get you started are, you could flip the property or sell the note or rent and hold. We'll talk more about this in the chapter on the exit strategies.

Building the vision

This is one of my favorite parts when going through this process. It's where you get to paint a detailed picture of the next 10 years and where you and your empire will be. Start in a new page in your business plan document and vividly describe what your business will look like in an ideal (but practical) way. Allow your imagination to take over and show you what's possible. Detail the purchases, cash flow, appreciation, trades, 1031 exchanges, cash-on-cash return and more. Make sure the goals you set, the mission statement and this vision align. You may not know how to get to the vision and chances are the path will not be straightforward but putting it down with as much clarity as possible is the first step toward making it a reality.

One last thing to remember here is that it doesn't have to be perfect and you shouldn't expect the journey to go exactly as planned on paper. It is good to have this detailed document, but you're bound to hit some obstacles along the way and experience some failure. As long as you remain flexible and focused on the long-term vision you defined for yourself, success will be inevitable.

Many investors who've experienced great failure attribute a considerable portion of it to lack of preparation and proper planning. Now you know how to avoid falling into the same trap.

How to invest with little or no money

I am super passionate about this part right here. Coming up with creative ways to run successful deals that turn a profit with no money to is what changed my life when I started out. I want to give you the nitty gritty on how you can invest in real estate without cash or credit.

If you want to make things happen, you'll need a couple of things.

First, you'll need to find the right deal. I have a whole section devoted to this so you'll find helpful tips on how to do this right if you're feeling overwhelmed. Just know, there is a surplus of deals right where you are and with the right mindset and a lot of research you can find one that sets you on the highway to success.

Second, you need to have the right knowledge because if you're not knowledgeable in real estate, you won't get very far. There is no cheating in this industry, those with more knowledge and people skills always come out as winners no matter what anyone else tells you. For those starting out low on cash, this part becomes even more critical as it can become the one thing that gives you an edge and causes an investor to go all in on you and your deals. Do whatever it takes to acquire the right knowledge and continue to learn as much as you can about this industry.

Third, you need to create a way of funding the deals by bringing in someone who can bring in the money. Because when dealing with real estate investing, it does take money. It always takes money; anyone who tells you different is only revealing their lack of expertise in this industry. But the good news is that it doesn't have to be your money.

The best way I've found to make a lot of money when starting from scratch is to either do a lease option or build a relationship with a partner (with a 50-50 agreement) where they bring in the credit and cash, and you run the deals, bring the knowledge, organize a solid team, etc. By leveraging your skills and ability to get awesome deals in play, any good partner with money who wants to become wealthy as well should be more than happy to form a partnership with you.

Kris Krohn pays a great testament to how brilliant this strategy of forming partnerships can be and in fact, said that he made his first million dollars with less than ten thousand dollars of his own cash.

In our world, with the kind of technology today we have available today, finding the money is actually easier than you think. And although I will be talking more about how to fund and finance your deals, here's a great example to copy and paste right now.

Hrishab Bandopadh decided to forge his path to financial freedom by investing in real estate. The only problem was, he had zero cash to fund it and didn't even own a credit card. What he did have was a lot of knowledge and a knack for finding really hot deals. So when he started doing his research, he used a very cool tactic that most self-made real estate investors know about. He went into Facebook and joined all the relevant groups he could find of people just like him that we're looking to build wealth using real estate. It took him about six months of actual relationship building, but in the end, he was able to connect with a guy who partnered with him on his first deal. The rest, as they say, is history.

Today, he says getting into real estate was one of the best decisions he ever made. And as an immigrant who came to America to live the dream, he feels he's definitely found his path. Hrishab especially likes the lease option and says most of his success can be attributed to this method of rent to own homes. He and his partner get these homes for 300% less than market value from and then sells them for their real price.

Think about how different your life can be a few months from now if you can start working on this today. It doesn't matter how old you are, how much money you have or what job you do, making money investing in real estate can be is no longer just a wish, it can become your reality.

Now, if you feel pumped up and ready to get out there, then it's time to dive deep and figure out the best real estate for you to invest in.

Chapter 05: The Best Type Of Real Estate Niches For You To Invest In

Have you ever walked into an ice-cream parlor on a hot summer afternoon eager to get some ice cream only to feel a bit overwhelmed and confused by the number of choices there are? If you ever walk into an Italian ice-cream parlor, the endless options of homemade ice cream will make it tough to choose which scoop to order. The better option sometimes is just to ask to taste as many of the flavors as possible to discover the best one for you. It saves you having to order too many scoops and keeps you from overindulging and feeling guilty afterward for too much calorie intake.

While this is a trivial example, real estate investing is often times the same. There are so many options you could get into, and it might seem like its a good idea to know everything there is about the industry, but in reality, you don't need to know it all, you need to get good at the one or two niches that feel like a perfect fit. Some people know these things intuitively. Others need to test and experiment before honing down on a niche. There is no right or wrong here but let me remind you, getting your niche will be more profitable for you. Don't try to be a jack-of-all-trades. Remember when we said real estate investing is the vehicle taking you to your desired destination of financial freedom and early retirement? Sticking to one vehicle is wise, and that comes from honing down a niche that feels best for you.

Following is a list that includes the most popular property types that real estate investors deal with. You could get even more granular with each of these types if you wanted to. Keep in mind it is not necessary to master them all. This is just an overview to help you understand the options available for you so you can make an informed decision.

Key point: The sooner you can identify a niche that feels right for you, the easier it becomes to establish yourself as a trusted authority and expert. Narrow down your focus as you go through this list, start networking within this niche and execute on your plan of action.

Single family

Many beginners consider single-family homes as the best first step in real estate investing. They are relatively easy to rent, sell and finance. But just because they are easy to get started on doesn't mean you should blindly jump in. Do your market research well; make sure the deal is a profitable, cash flow favorable deal.

The biggest issue with single-family houses especially in certain markets is the fact that the rents derived from a single-family rental (SFR) may not be ample to provide a positive cash flow. Stay away from any deal if the numbers aren't right. Cash flow is your ticket to building wealth and retiring early. Where there's no positive cash flow, walk away quickly.

Small multifamily

These are usually 2 - 4 units. They are often just as easy as the single-family home when it comes to financing and selling and when bought properly, these can produce a good amount of cash flow. They also have less bidding competition in comparison to single-family homes.

One of the upsides of purchasing a small multifamily home is that you only need one loan and if you are a smart buyer, this can turn into a solid investment as well as your personal residence. As a beginner, I recommend focusing on three types of multifamily properties: the duplex, triplex, and fourplex (four units). These types offer the most upside with the least amount of risk for those just getting started in real estate investing and they are also more affordable.

Small Apartments

Investing in large multifamily properties will boost your income while reducing vacancy rates and is, therefore, a more profitable investment strategy for those who know what they are doing. This will require a reasonable amount of due diligence and hustle in comparison to smaller properties, but the cash flow potential is worth the effort.

These are usually small apartment buildings comprising anything between 5 - 50 units. These types of properties rely on commercial lending standards rather than residential ones, but if you can deal with added responsibility that comes with managing these properties, you will generate a much higher return on investment and cash flow.

It's also worth mentioning that these types of properties usually have less competition because on the one hand they are too small for big professional Real Estate Investment Trust (REITs), and on the other are too large for most amateur real estate investors.

Another unique attribute to these types of properties is they are not being priced based on comparable properties aka "comps." Instead, they are evaluated based on the income they bring in which means there's an excellent opportunity to add value by increasing rent, decreasing expenses and managing the property effectively. One cool tactic to use here would be to get great on-site managers who help you manage and perform maintenance in exchange for decreased or free rental space.

Large Apartments

These types of properties are large complexes often with pools, gym facilities, full-time staff, and high advertising budgets. Such properties can cost millions, so this is probably not going to be the best starting point for any self-made real estate investor with little to no cash, but it's still worth knowing that you can invest in it as you build your portfolio.

This class of property although highly priced can produce stable returns with minimal personal involvement which makes it great as a stream of passive income. Many large apartments are owned by a small group of investors (syndicates) who pool their resources. Therefore the more you become a trusted authority and expert, your ability to network, find the right investors and create or join syndication can move you closer to owning these types of properties.

Mobile homes

Mobile homes can be a good investment for a beginner, and they require little money out of pocket. This could be a home in a mobile home park or on its own land. Many of the strategies used in the other popular types of real estate investing can be applied to mobile homes as well so don't be shy to experiment with this type of investing if it strikes your interest.

Commercial

Unless you have a healthy financial situation, I don't advice investing in commercial real estate. Although they can be quite lucrative, they also carry enormous risks and a heavy responsibility. As a beginner, it's good to learn about commercial real estate especially if that is your ultimate goal but take your time investing in this niche.

The purpose, style, and size of a commercial real estate property will vary greatly, but ultimately all commercial properties are leased to some kind of small business. Some commercial investors will rent the building to small local businesses while others prefer to rent out large spaces to big-box megastores and supermarkets. Either way, these types of investments usually provide good cash flow and excellent ROI. There is a downside however that every investor needs to be aware of. These properties often have a more extended holding period sometimes sitting vacant for many months or even years during which time your cash flow disappears. So before investing in this niche market, do a self-check to make sure your finances can handle it.

Raw Land

This niche is for those who would like to own a piece of earth and turn it into a business. Land, on its own, can be improved and then leased out or rented to generate positive cash flow. You could also subdivide it and sell portions or all of it for profit. Some real estate investors like to purchase raw land with the plan of selling it someday for external developments such as a housing development or construction of a freeway.

Private Notes

This type of investment is about buying and selling paper mortgages. Here's what I mean. Imagine you purchased a home with a loan. In that case, a "note" was created detailing the terms of the contract. Now let's assume you decided to sell your property for one million dollars and you offer to carry the full note (thus allowing the new buyer to avoid using a bank loan), enabling the new buyer to make payments of eight percent per year for thirty years until the full one million dollars is paid off.

If at some point you decide that you no longer want to be involved, you can choose to sell the mortgage to a note buyer. The note buyer will then begin collecting the monthly mortgage payments and keep the note or sell it again in the future.

Tax Liens

This opportunity comes about when a homeowner doesn't pay their taxes. In such a situation, the government (local state or federal) has the power to foreclose the home and then resell the property to investors for the amount owed. Generally, this tends to be an incredibly underpriced value making it an inexpensive purchase, which is great if the actual home is a good deal. So don't just blindly chase after deals like these ones. Do your due diligence, crunch the numbers and make sure the home is cash flow positive before jumping into this kind of investing. Tax lien sales are often very complex transactions and require lots of knowledge, experience, and research.

REITs

A real estate investment trusts (REIT) is an alliance that is formed by a large number of individuals who pool their funds together to create what is known as a REIT. This alliance makes it possible for them to purchase huge real estate investments. I'm talking about large apartment complexes, skyscrapers, shopping malls or even bulk amounts of single-family homes.

The process involves buying shares from a company or corporation that owns the real estate properties and then waiting to receive dividends as income. Keep in mind this income isn't tax exempt so you would need to pay taxes.

If you were to become part of such an alliance, the REIT would distribute profit to you and all the other investors. It is one of the best ways to generate passive income and have a hands-off approach to real estate investing as you build your portfolio. However, you should know the ROI isn't usually as high as being hands-on and managing your own investments fully. If you would like to buy shares in a REIT, simply do it via your stock account.

This list is far from exhausted but what you've learned so far are the most popular niches you can get into immediately as you build your portfolio in this industry. Again, my recommendation is to start with one or two niches and gain mastery on them. Build a credible name for yourself then expand as your income, experience, knowledge, and resources expand.

Now, let's talk strategy so that you can get the most out of your chosen niche.

Chapter 06: The Best Type Of Real Estate Strategies

These are the most common strategies to make money with real estate. I have focused mostly on strategies that any new investor can leverage regardless of their financial situation. Bear in mind that in this section our emphasis will be on profitable strategies that are time tested and proven to work even for people with no prior experience.

House Flipping

Flipping houses has become a very popular practice. Perhaps it has something to do with the numerous cable television shows promoting it. Regardless of why it's becoming so popular, house flipping is a strategy I recommend testing out if it resonates with you.

It involves buying a piece of real estate at a discounted price, adding value by improving it in some way and then selling it for a profit. A similar model to help you envision this is the standard retail model of "buy low, sell high."

Since the single-family home tends to be the easiest to buy in real estate, it's the most popular type of property to use this strategy on. When it comes to house flipping, there's a rule of thumb known as the 70% rule. A seventy percent rule means an experienced house flipper will buy a home for 70% of its current (minus any rehabilitation costs).

For example. A home is worth $250,000 if it was in perfect conditions, but it needs $35,000 worth of rehabilitation work. An experienced house flipper would be able to purchase this home for $175,000 ($250,000 X 70% - $35,000) and seek to sell it for the full $250,000 once the rehabilitation work is completed.

Please note this is merely a rule of thumb and actual numbers verified and adjusted to ensure a profitable and successful flip.

Avoid this mistake:

Don't make the mistake of assuming this is a passive income strategy. House flipping requires effort and active, hands-on participation as well as speed and efficiency if you want to make money from it. In essence, it is like having a job because you only make money when you flip a house.

Speed is essential when it comes to house flipping. You need to buy, rehabilitate and sell the property as fast as possible to ensure maximum profit and to avoid many months of expensive costs like property taxes, utilities, financing charges, condo fees (where applicable) and any other maintenance bills required to keep the house in good physical or financial standing.

Wholesaling

This is a strategy few people know about, and even fewer teach it well. And when done right it can literally launch you into your first millions with no cash down.

Technically speaking, wholesaling is a process that requires you to run a deal without ever owning the piece of property you're attempting to sell. Sounds confusing right? Let me see if I can simplify it more.

The wholesaling process involves finding really great deals, writing a contract to acquire the deal and selling the contract to another buyer and receiving what we call an assignment fee. This fee typically ranges between $500 - $5,000 and higher depending on the size of the deal. In other words, it's about being a middleman who gets paid for finding great deals.

A wholesaler is really great at marketing and finding incredible deals. As a wholesaler, you can sell your contracts to retail buyers or to other investors such as house flippers who are usually cash buyers. This strategy requires someone with strong people skills and someone who is willing to go the extra mile to build solid relationships and credibility within the real estate community. And because most of the buyers are cash buyers, you'll often get paid within days or weeks. It is most definitely a low entry barrier especially if you don't have money to start investing and you can quickly get the experience and connections (not to mention make some real money). Many real estate gurus enjoy promoting this strategy. But do not be fooled, this isn't a magic bullet. You still need to put in the effort and have the right knowledge. And you need to be good at winning people's trust.

Avoid this mistake:

Don't approach this with the "lazy man's mindset." It's not just about finding buyers, it's also about being really good at spotting great deals and motivated sellers who are willing to trust you. Your marketing won't just take care of itself, you've got to be super proactive, and even though anyone can do wholesaling, those who are well equipped with strong marketing funnels are the ones who grow and scale their businesses faster.

If you chose to go with this strategy, be persistent, increase your people skills and wholesaling knowledge, and you will generate a good income stream while you continue to master other more profitable forms of investing.

House hacking

House hacking is a strategy many newbie investors are leveraging when they first enter the real estate arena. It involves purchasing a two, three or four unit property then living in one unit and renting out the others.

Most people will start off with a single-family house when they invest in real estate but smart investors who understand the importance of cash flow follow a different route.

By investing in at least a duplex, you minimize the possibility of becoming a slave to your house expenses such as mortgage, taxes repair and maintenance costs.

The benefit of doing a house hacking strategy is that when done right you could actually live for free. Your property will produce cash flow for you as it continues to appreciate over time.

For example. You could buy a quadplex, live in one of the units and rent out the rest. Since it's still considered a residential unit, you only need to get one loan to cover it, and if you crunch your numbers right and find the right deal, you can end up with a property that pays for all your expenses.

Avoid this mistake:

Don't jump into a deal too soon. Take your time and do as much research as possible to find the ideal one for you that produces enough cash flow to cover your costs. You also need to make sure you vet the tenants thoroughly and implement policies and procedures that protect you and your family in case something goes wrong with the tenants. Most novice real estate investors forget to take these precautionary steps, and it ends up costing them a lot financially and legally.

Live-In-House Flips

This strategy works best for an investor who is very patient, doesn't mind living in a construction zone and also enjoys DIY projects. It is a very hands-on type of real estate investing, but some have enjoyed enormous profits doing it.

Live in house flipping involves purchasing a home that requires a lot of rehabilitation, fixing it while living in it full time and then selling it for a profit.

One of the main benefits of doing this is that when done right, there are no income taxes imposed. Live-in house flipping exempts owners from paying capital gains taxes on the sale up to $250,000 for an individual and $500,000 for a couple as long as they've lived at the property for at least two of the previous five years.

Avoid this mistake:

Don't get into live-in-house flips if you don't understand construction and contractors. Too many people are blindsided by issues like termites or cracks in the foundation, which can only be overcome when one has sufficient knowledge and understanding of how construction works. You also need to have an eye for good property deals so that you can get one that will sell well when the time comes.

Lastly, don't jump into this strategy unless you have a reasonable budget in place, cash reserves and a lot of patience. Sometimes the construction work needed may take longer than expected, or the house may not sell when you want it to sell, and you need to be okay with keeping money tied up until then.

Student rentals

Using this strategy won't be glamorous, but it can be very lucrative. Student rental investing is about providing students a great place to live when they leave home and making a significant income in the process. They often give a robust cash flow. You could buy a house for $300,000 and generate $3,500 per month in rental income because in many cases you could have even seven students living in a house paying $500 per room.

One of the major challenges to this otherwise lucrative strategy is the lease. You need to make sure you keep a single contract in place so that the student house doesn't become a rooming house. Which means although there are many rents to be collected each month, they need to be carried under a single lease and with technology, there are lots of simple processes in place to help with this, but you still need to be hands-on for this strategy to work.

Avoid this mistake:

Don't get lured in by the cash flow this strategy generates. Make sure you understand all the financing and legislation aspects required to make this strategy a success. Each city usually has different legislation detailing how it zones these types of dwelling. Some will regulate the number of students per house and also have rules on maintenance, fire safety standards, insurance, parking, noise, etc.

Some cities license student housing at around $500 for the first year and then it drops slightly for subsequent years. There's no denying, this strategy is time-consuming and needs a hands-on approach because most of the students will keep calling for assistance so do your due diligence and become aware of all your costs and responsibilities before jumping in.

Buy and Hold

I consider this to be one of the purest forms of real estate investing. It involves purchasing a property, renting it out for an extended period and eventually selling it for profit. If you invest in a buy and hold strategy, the primary objective would be to rent out the purchased property to collect a monthly cash flow and then eventually selling it out in future profitably.

One of the benefits of using this strategy (if you're doing it right) is that the mortgage on the property will pay itself out through the monthly cash flow generated decreasing your principal balance and increasing your equity over time.

Avoid this mistake:

Don't buy deals that don't yield a positive cash flow. Learn to evaluate properties thoroughly and avoid making the same mistake made by many new investors make. Every decision you make including managing your expenses, choosing the right tenant, managing your assets are all crucial to your success. If done poorly they can result in significant loses. But these are all mistakes that can be avoided with the right knowledge.

There is also a real estate marketing cycle that you need to understand and leverage when making your buy-and-hold decisions.

Every market will be different. You need to identify the ebbs and flow of the marketplace where your property is located. Then you need to increase your education, learn to evaluate properties, find good deals and great tenants.

Short Term Rentals

Short-term rentals are very alluring. They are actually considered the fast way of making money in real estate. This is the Airbnb style of real estate investing where you purchase a property and rent it out on a short-term basis. Usually, the rents are very high, and if your property is in a touristic location, you could charge higher rents and expect to be booked out for most of the year.

Because you're here as a beginner in real estate investing, it's important to remind you that location is everything if you're going to go for this strategy.

The main reason Airbnb properties do so well is they serve as a substitute for hotels and motels. There is also a lot of direct contact between the host/owner and the tenants. Offering a unique and unforgettable experience to your guests is what will help you grow a thriving business with short term rentals so you'll need to either prepare yourself to be more hands-on or hire some professional help.

One more thing you also need to keep in mind is the increased competition from other landlords doing the same, as well as the high turnover of renters who only occupy the place for short durations.

Avoid this mistake:

Get clarity on the type of real estate investor you want to be. If long term, consistent passive income is what you're after, and you want optimal results then don't get into short-term rentals expecting such results. This strategy is not for everyone, and usually, the more dynamic investor looking for short-term gain in real estate is the type who will enjoy this strategy. Get educated on what makes Airbnb properties successful and make sure you're willing to go all in and deliver in both tangible and intangible ways to the clientele that need short term rentals.

Turnkey Investing

This investment strategy has a longer learning curve and can be scary for some, but if you acquire the right knowledge, the benefits of turnkey investing are fantastic. When you hear real estate gurus talking about passive income and getting real estate to work for you, this is one of those strategies that can help you accomplish all that and more. Passive income is the primary objective of investing in a turnkey property.

This strategy is actually straightforward and can be quite flexible, but the ultimate concept behind turnkey is that you as an investor don't need to be hands-on with the investment. Your role is to "turn the key" on a piece of property and make good money from it.

Some investors consider turnkey investing as a property that is already fixed and rented with a third party company managing it. In such as a case all that the investor does is make the investment and get paid any profit.

Other investors consider turnkey investing to be a property that might need some rehabilitation. In such a case the investor would need to fix it up a bit, maybe even find tenants to rent but then turn the management over to someone else. At that point, the investor would sit on the sidelines collecting income from the investment without having to deal with the day-to-day operations.

You get to define what "turnkey investing" will mean for you. Regardless of how you define it, there are two components to always bear in mind.

1. A turnkey investment property is usually not a local property. Turnkey means the amount of effort you put into the investment is minimal especially once the property is rent ready.

2. Your opportunities for investing are unlimited because you can buy the property anywhere.

A major benefit of not being limited to local real estate investing is that you can access areas where houses are for sale for less money. You will be able to buy a property for less, make the property better and then get income from it. And the best part is this strategy allows you to step away from all the work required to own and manage a property (which is usually a full-time job), and just make money. If you do your research well and partner up with the right turnkey real estate company, they might even buy the house first, clean it up and then sell it to you. They make their money by managing it, and you own the property.

Avoid this mistake:

Try not to buy a property without seeing it or knowing its real potential. Understandably, the fact that the property could be a long distance away from you might make it hard for you to personally vet the property. But I still argue against it. Some real estate investors do this, and it's such a gamble. It could work out well, or it could end up being a lemon that costs more money than it makes.

There are always risks involved with any real estate investing but blindly jumping into a deal merely because it's a turnkey investment opportunity is a grievous mistake that's unnecessary. Smart real estate investors do everything possible to gain as much first-hand knowledge of the property before making an investment. I recommend you always do the same even with this strategy.

All the strategies we've shared work. The one best suited for you depends entirely on your objectives, personality and your "WHY." The business plan we created in an earlier chapter will guide you into choosing the right strategy because you'll see which one aligns perfectly with that road map that you created for yourself. This is a decision you need to make for yourself based on how much effort you want to put into growing your real estate business. Now that you're well on your way to your first deal let's get into the mathematics and financing so we can ensure this activity leads you to financial freedom.

Chapter 07: Financing Your Investments

Are you eager to start growing your real estate business but fear it can't happen because you're low on cash?

Let's face it, not everyone is as fortunate as Donald Trump to have a wealthy, well-connected dad who makes the launching of a successful real estate career easy.

Most of us have to start with the little crumbs we can gather, and it's a slow boat to China. But the good news is, despite the limited resources anyone (and I mean you) can get started in real estate investing.

While you can become a real estate investor with no money down, the truth is, money is always involved in a real estate transaction. So one way or another, you have to figure out how to come up with money that isn't yours to make your first deal happen. If it's not your own money, then it will be other people's money. There's a skill required to make you good at getting people to buy into your ideas and give you their money. The more you develop that skill, the faster your real estate business will take off.

Know your numbers

Regardless of what infomercials and hyped up online marketers lead you to believe, there's no such thing as free real estate. It's worth reiterating that over and over again to avoid entering the game with the wrong mindset. Real estate is a commodity, and it must be paid for.

And if you want to get the most out of any deal and leverage the best tool for financing, you first need to know your numbers. Without knowing the math behind your deals, you're flying blind. You must be on top of your debt, you need to know your margins, and you need to calculate operating expenses and determine your return even before making that first purchase. So how well do you know the real estate numbers?

I gave you the basic terminology that you must know in chapter two, and at the end of this book you'll find a more comprehensive glossary to equip you with real estate language know-how, but you still need to educate yourself on the necessary mathematics.

Here are thirteen real estate investing numbers you need to know.

1. Your Mortgage Payment:

For a standard owner-occupied home, lenders typically prefer a total debt-to-income ratio of 36%, but some will go to 45% depending on other qualifying factors such as cash reserves or your credit score. This ratio compares your total gross monthly income with your monthly debt payment obligations.

For housing payment, lenders prefer a gross income-to-total housing payment of 28 to 33%, depending on other factors. For an investment property aim for a maximum debt-to-income ratio of 45%

2. Down Payment Requirements

Owner-occupied properties can be financed with a mortgage and as little as 3.5% down for an FHA loan (see glossary for definition). Investor mortgages however vary and typically require a down payment of 20 to 25% or sometimes as much as 40%. None of the down payment or closing costs for an investment property should come from gift funds.

Individual lenders will determine how much you need to put down to qualify for a loan depending on your debt-to-income ratios, credit score, the property price, and potential rent.

3. Price to Income Ratio

This ratio compares the median household price in an area to the median household income. Before the housing bubble burst, the price-to-income ratio in the U.S was 2.75. By the end of 2010, the ratio was 1.71.

4. Rental Income to Qualify

Most new investors assume that since the tenant's rent payment will cover the mortgage, they don't need extra income to qualify for the home loan. However, this isn't accurate. For the rent to qualify as income, you must have a two-year history of managing investment properties. You also need to purchase rent loss insurance coverage for at least six months of gross monthly rent, and any negative rental income from any rental property must be considered as debt in the debt-to-income ratio.

5. Price to Rent Ratio

This is a calculation that compares median home prices and median rents in a particular market. To do this, divide the median house price by the median annual rent to generate a ratio.

At the peak of the U.S market in 2006, the ratio for the U.S was 18.46. The ratio dropped to 11.34 by the end of 2010. The long-term average between 1989-2003 was 9.56.

As a general rule of thumb, consumers usually buy when the ratio is under 15 and rent when it's above 20. Markets with a high price/rent ratio typically aren't considered great investment opportunities.

6. Gross Rental Yield

The gross rental yield for a property can be found by dividing the annual rent collected by the total property cost, then multiplying that number by 100 to get the percentage. The total property cost includes the purchase price, all closing costs, and rehabilitation costs.

(Annual rent collected/total property cost) * 100

7. Capitalization Rate

This number is probably even more valuable than the gross rental yield. Mostly referred to as the cap rate or net rental yield, this figure includes all operating expenses for the property. You can calculate this by taking your annual rent, subtracting your annual expenses, then dividing that number by the total property cost and lastly, multiplying the resulting number by 100 for the percentage.

[(Annual rent - annual expenses)/total property costs] * 100
Included in the total rental property expenses are repair costs, landlord insurance, taxes, vacancy costs, and agent fees.

8. Calculating Operating expenses:

Operating expenses on your new property will be between 35% and 80% of your gross operating income (see glossary for definition). For example, if on your first deal you charge $1,500 for rent and your expenses are $600 per month, you're at 40%

You may also use the 50% rule. If your rent charge is $3,000 per month, expect to pay $1500 in total expenses.

9. Calculating your margins:

As an individual investor, I recommend setting a goal of 10%. Estimate costs at 1% of the property value annually. And don't forget to include things such as insurance, property taxes, monthly expenses such as pest control and landscaping. There's also the landlord insurance where applicable and homeowners association fees.

10. Cash flow

To set yourself on the path of riches as a landlord you need to be able to cover the mortgage principal, interest, taxes, and insurance with the monthly rent. You also need to have cash reserves at hand ready to cover that payment in case you have a vacancy or need to cover unexpected maintenance costs.

Avoid negative cash flow. This usually occurs if you borrow too much to buy the property.

11. After Repair Value

This is simply the value of your property subject to any proposed repairs. Rehabilitating a property inherently increases its value. To calculate how much your proposed renovations may increase your home's value you must dive into some research. Find comparable homes that have recently sold and were in a condition similar to your property's condition and the rehab is done.

12. Repair Budget

For an investment to be successful, you must make and stick to your rehabilitation budget. The budget should reflect all necessary repairs to make your home's condition comparable to those properties in which you used to determine your after repair value (ARV). You need to move fast, create a cheat-sheet for your rehab cost and use round estimates for large items like kitchens, bathrooms, paint, and flooring.

13. Purchase Price

This is also called an offer price. It's essential to making a sound investment because if the offering is too low, you might get outbid and if your offer is too high, you might kill your profit margins.

I recommend you reverse engineer this process. Start by determining your desired return and then subtracting that return and any associated costs from the after repair value (ARV). The resulting figure should essentially reflect your initial offer price.

Now that you've made all these calculation, you're in a better position to make an informed decision about whether a particular property will be a valuable investment so let's move on to how you actually finance the deal.

How to finance your deals

Here are a variety of options for you to finance your first deal as you grow your real estate business.

1. Funding from friends and family

Do you know what Warren Buffet and World Trade Center developer Larry Silverstein have in common?

They both became billionaires after financing their first deals through family and friends. Yes, you read it right. They started small, with the resources available to them and the best part about their strategy is that anyone can do it.

Silverstein actually shared some of his story in a recent interview where he said they were not doing well financially. Silverstein and his father were brokers, which made them very little money. He got tired of living off scraps and told his father they needed to find a way out and become owners; otherwise, they would end up starving to death. Having realized that owners are the ones who make money in real estate, Silverstein and his father made their first acquisition of a distressed Manhattan property by pooling money from 20 people. The Silverstein closed the deal on the building, cleaned it up, refinanced it and paid investors back (plus profit), setting the foundation of what would become one of the biggest real estate fortunes today.

You don't need any startup capital, credit or any of the other criterions everyone else wants. You just need to be good at getting your friends and family to have faith in you.

And in the U.S it's even easier than you think to get friends and family to help you finance your first deal. Get 10 family members to go to FHA (you'll learn what this is below), and have them pool less than $1000, which will allow you to pick up a multifamily property. From there, apply one of the strategies we shared, and you'll be on your way to building your real estate fortune.

2. Trust Deed Investing

This isn't too far from the first tip of family and friends because it's also built on trust. By using this method, you're essentially taking a mortgage from one or more private lenders who would function as a bank, giving them a deed of trust as collateral on the property.

In other words, you commit to meeting the lending terms given to you and if you don't, the private lender (like a regular bank) has the right to foreclose the property should you not meet the terms agreed upon.

More and more real estate investors are choosing this approach offering 8% - 10% APR to lenders to invest in deals with high profit.

3. Federal Housing Administration (FHA) Loans

In the United States, there is a government program that insures mortgages for banks. If you have health or car insurance you probably already understand this concept. It's about pooling money to spread the risk for everyone. The Federal Housing Administrative loan can be a sound way to go about making your first deal happen because, with a small down payment of 3.5%, you could quickly pick up a multifamily property, live in one of the units and rent out the other units producing cash flow while the property appreciates over time.

FHA loans are designed only for homeowners who are going to live in the property so you cannot use an FHA-backed loan to buy a property purely as an investment. Which is why I've suggested getting a multifamily property.

One of the main benefits of financing your first deal this way is that you get to make a little down payment. It's a quick way to get started. However, the downside to this method is that an FHA loan requires additional payments to be made known as Private Mortgage Insurance (PMI). This is a type of insurance that protects the lender and is needed whenever a down payment is less than 20%.

Having a PMI makes your monthly payment slightly higher thus reducing your positive cash flow, but with the juicy income you'll get while holding the property, you could efficiently manage to cover all payments and expenses basically living rent-free while the property pays for itself. Just be sure to find a great deal that produces positive cash flow.

Logan Allec from California shared his success story and how he got started on his first deal in his 20s by using an FHA loan. His first property was a fourplex in a suburb of Los Angeles. It was financed using an FHA loan whereby he put the 3.5% down payment on a purchase price of $435,000 with a $15,000 seller credit. Keep in mind when he got started he didn't have tons of cash in the bank. In fact, he was still paying off student loans but was able to pull this off with just a little hustle and proper education.

He lived in one of the four units and rented out the other three. Since he was young and single, he also rented out the bedroom in his unit and slept on a mattress in the living room. This is what's known as "house hacking," and in chapter six I showed you how to leverage the same strategy if it aligns with your goals. Allec essentially combined a couple of strategies together and ended up living for free, building his equity and generating cash flow for a mere $15,000 out of pocket.

If you're low on cash, whether you're a young millennial or not, this might be the no brainer way to finance your first deal. But let's keep moving on and address other ways you could fund your next deal.

4. Hard Money

This refers to financing that is obtained from a private business or an individual for the purpose of investing in real estate. They usually have higher interest rates, but they give you the flexibility to strike quickly if you have a fantastic deal ready to go. Traditional mortgages are often quite slow and may take around two months or more to close (a very long time if you need to close a deal fast).

I don't consider this a sustainable long-term option for financing your deals, but it is a viable resource when you're starting from scratch with no connections or support, and you come across a killer deal. While the terms and style of this type of financing may vary, there are a few defining characteristics to be aware of:

• This is usually a short-term loan (due in 6 - 36 months).

- The loan is primarily based on the value of the property.

- The interest rates are generally higher (8 - 15%).

- Hard money does not show on your personal credit report.

- Many hard money lenders do not require income verification.

- Many hard money lenders do not require credit references.

- Hard money can often fund a deal in a matter of days making it super fast to close deals.

- Hard moneylenders usually understand when the property needs rehabilitation work.

If you're wondering how to find a hard moneylender, try the following.

Ask a house flipper.

Ask a real estate agent.

Ask a mortgage broker.

Google it.

Use Craigslist.

Remember short-term loans can be tricky. Make sure you understand the implications of using this method to finance it, including all the risks involved with your particular deal.

5. Owner Financing

Banks and other giant lending institutions are not the only entities that can finance your deal. Did you know that?

In some cases, the owner of the property you want to buy can actually fund the purchase.

This is the Holy Grail especially for those of us starting out with no funds. If you can do an owner financing, all you need to do is make monthly payments to the seller rather than a bank.

Getting this type of a deal would be like striking gold on the first try. They are usually not easy to come by, but it's not impossible. Often, a property owner will do this for you if they own the home free and clear (they have no existing mortgage on the property) and they want out.

One thing to be cautious about while using this method is to find out whether the owner of the property has an ongoing loan. If the seller does have another loan when selling the home to you, that loan needs to be paid back immediately otherwise you risk bank foreclosure. There's a legal clause written into nearly every loan called the due on sale clause, which gives the former lender the right to call the note immediately due. If the amount can't be paid, then the lender has the right to foreclose on the property. So while owner financing can be a great way to gain ownership of real estate without using a bank, be sure to do some due diligence before signing off on the deal.

6. Buy-2-rent: The Asset-Based Mortgage

Still struggling to come to terms with using hard moneylenders and non-bank agreements? Well, there are other ways to get a deal that is worth mentioning. Asset-based mortgages are one such tool you could use to finance your first deal. Buy 2 rent is a mortgage product from Blackstone-owned B2R Finance and they mainly look at the rental income the property will produce. Unlike traditional banks, this mortgage product doesn't look at personal income (which is great if you don't have a stable income), but they do require a 660 FICO score and other underwriting criteria.

I consider B2R's product an alternative to hard money loans and traditional financing, and since it's based on rental income, it's perfect for real estate investors who are just starting out. By financing your first deal this way, you can get up to 80% LTV for an acquisition or up to 75% for a refinancing. Interest rates range from 6% - 8% giving your start-up a real opportunity to close on properties.

Another great advantage of using B2R is the fact that you have more flexibility and aren't limited on the number of properties you can invest in hence growing your portfolio becomes easier, and you'll never have to deal with traditional financing.

7. Partnerships

Partnerships are a great way to finance a deal, especially when starting out. If you find a really great deal but the price range is beyond your current reach, getting an equity partner might be a better move. You can build a team and bring on an equity partner (someone you trust and bring into a deal to help finance it).

There's no one size fits all when it comes to structuring a partnership. It's something you and your partner will have to agree. You can use the partner's cash to finance the entire property, or they can only fund the down payment. There are no set rules but what you do need is to make a decision on how the deal will be put together, who will make the decisions and how profits will be split at the end.

James Walton, a real estate investor, now closing in on his third year as a full-time real estate investor, says during his first year, after gaining some momentum, he came across an incredible deal that was too good to pass on. He lacked sufficient financing to go at it alone and thankfully, his father in law had been interested in real estate investing. So he became his first business partner agreeing on a 50-50 partnership.

Walton brought the knowledge, experience, and deals and he was in charge of putting the whole thing together. His father in law brought financing and credit. Two years in and now they've done almost a dozen deals together. Not too shabby for a guy who had no experience a few years ago.

If you can find a partner like Walton's father in law, you could quickly build your portfolio within the next twelve months. Depending on your operating agreement, your partner may have an active or passive role, and they may participate in nearly all aspects of the property ownership. An equity partner usually receives a percentage return on their investment that includes cash flow and profit when the property is sold. Unlike private lenders, an equity partnership does not receive an agreed upon interest rate on the loan because they get a percentage of generated income instead. If the property makes a lot of money, then their return will be higher. If the investment loses money, they may have to continue financing to keep the property running until things turn around.

Equity partners take a higher risk than private lenders, but they also have higher returns if the investment is successful.

8. Hybrid Financing: Equity Mixed with Debt

This can come across as complex, but I will do my best to simplify it. Let's assume you have an excellent deal and now you have a gap to fill because you've got 75% of the LTV (checkglossary for definition), but you need to come up with the remaining 25% assuming you don't have the cash in hand.

A creative way of handling this problem would be taking out a hybrid loan. Mix the traditional payment schedule of a mortgage with a piece of equity for the lender. But you need to know what you're doing, and you must do your due diligence to ensure you're not dealing with scam lenders and that what you offer them is valuable to them.

The last thing you want is to waste everyone's time by stacking up a hybrid that doesn't make sense to your lenders. Even though private money and mezzanine equity are highly flexible, they also tend to stick to their niches. You have to know what your capital providers specialize in so that you can pick one that will be comfortable if your particular case.

In some deals, you may end up paying a higher rate or give up some control possibly even granting them permission to be active in the investment, but if you do it right and the deal makes sense, you'll end up with a win-win situation.

9. Private Money

Private money lending is similar to hard money in many respects, but it's usually distinguishable due to the relationship between the lender and the borrower. This one is all about relationship building. The better the relationship, the more effective this method will be. In general, the private moneylender will not be a professional like a hard money lender. He or she is usually an individual looking to achieve higher returns on their cash. These types of lenders are generally not business-oriented (at least not like hard money lenders) and the entire agreement is built on a relationship with the borrower.

A private lender will lend you cash to buy the property in exchange for a specific interest rate; however they usually have fewer fees and points, and the term length can be negotiated more easily. This ensures both parties have a win-win situation. When they invest with you, that investment will be secured by a mortgage on the property or promissory note, which means if you don't pay, they can foreclose and take the home just as a bank loan, hard moneylender or other loan types would.

When it comes to interest rate, nothing is fixed. You'll establish that upfront with your private moneylender and the money will be lent for a specific period ranging anywhere from six months to thirty years.

Generally, one investor finances private moneyand he or she gets no equity stake or cash flow or future value outside of the pre-determined interest rate. However, as I said, everything depends on the agreement you make because private capital is extremely flexible.

This is a great approach when you feel confident that you can refinance the property after adding value and I recommend having multiple clearly defined exit strategies to ensure you don't fail to pay the private lender. Just as I cautioned with hard money, private money must be approached with caution, and you need to be sure that the deal is worth the risk.

When it comes to private capital, building relationships and having credibility is imperative. You will need visibility in some way, and you'll have to prove that you are an expert in your chosen niche.

If you want to leverage this approach, make sure you're creating opportunities to highlight your investing experience. Make sure you're growing your online and offline presence. Start a blog, get more active on relevant

Facebook groups, attend local real estate investment events, become a member of your local club. The options are endless, especially with today's socially connected world. The more you become a well-known expert; the easier it will be to attract the right private money lender.

Anson Young, a full-time real estate investor from Colorado, is a wholesaler and flipper who is currently working towards becoming a millionaire doing real estate says the funds 100% of his purchase and rehabilitation using private money.

He says, private money lenders typically care more about the deal than they care about your credit score. They want to know you have a solid track record and they want to feel protected by having the first deed of trust on the property, so a hard asset secures their money.

Young finds private moneylenders by either reaching out to his network to find people who want a good return on their money or by reaching out to already established private money lenders who are actively lending in my area. Credibility is everything according to Young. And he's found that chronicling his investment activities through social media is a massive boost as it consistently reminds people that he's in real estate and that he's a professional.

Realize that real estate investing is a relationship based business, and people are investing in you and your ability to execute successfully so anything you can do to build that trust will go a long way.

There are of course other ways for you to finance your deals, but if starting out with little to no cash in hand, I believe these tips will work in your favor and help you exponentially build your portfolio.

Now that you have the strategies and you know your numbers and how to finance them, it's time to talk about where to go to find great deals as well as how to analyze your first deal.

Chapter 08: Finding Incredible Deals

Finding incredible deals has nothing to do with the market and everything to do with the marketing. Most real estate investors who are just starting out fall short of great success because they fail to create a strong enough pipeline of deals. In other words, their marketing sucks. The fact of the matter is, when you have an incredible deal, financing it becomes the least of your worries.

Anyone with half a brain and a desire to make more money will be willing to at least partner with you if you can show them a deal of a lifetime. So although most people think money is the biggest obstacle in building a successful real estate business, I have found the real hurdle is getting a robust pipeline of amazing deals.

Every savvy real estate investor needs a process that leads to a successful result. Have you figured out what your process will be?

In this chapter, I want to help you overcome that obstacle as much as possible. To start us off, I want to share a simple system that Biggerpockets.com evangelizes. They even have an entire resource that you can download on their website to help you dive deeper into this system if it resonates with you.

The LAPS Funnel

This funnel represents a process detailing the journey you need to take each time you want to close a profitable deal. Leads - Analysis - Propose - Success is one of the most straightforward processes you can emulate to start closing great deals.

Leads:

You need to source channels that offer you consistent, high quality leads. With the rise of technology and social media, I recommend compiling a list that includes both offline and online channels. Your goal at this first phase is to get as many fresh leads as you can into your funnel and then filter them out until you're left with just a few hot deals.

For example, I might gather 1,500 - 2,000 leads and only end up buying one property. The raw leads are the top of the funnel and could be any potential lead coming from direct mail list provider, driving for dollars, FB paid ads, MLS or something else. Once I have the raw lead, I start the qualifying process so they can turn into a hot lead. Hot leads qualify for the next phase.

Analysis:

An accurate analysis of a deal will include the four quadrants. Income, cash flow, expenses, cash on cash return. You not only need to know these terms and what they represent but you also need to run the calculations on each of them before signing off on any deal. For any property, there is a value that will make it worth buying and your job is to discover that magic number through a detailed analysis of the property. You also need to conduct a preliminary title search to make sure the property may be sold.

Analysis requires massive action, lots of research and enough knowledge about the market and this industry as a whole. While I may have started with up to 2,000 fresh leads which narrowed down to 100 hot leads, I might only analyze half of them (50 properties). So if you're not willing to put in the hustle, your efforts will fall short here, making it tough for you to find the right deals that will set up a foundation of success for your business. Do not shortcut this step while going through the process.

One of the key benefits of doing a thorough analysis and knowing your numbers is that you get to avoid falling for bad deals that look good on the surface.

For example, suppose you found a deal that was asking for $250,000 for a duplex. While doing your analysis, you realize it would take $200,000 to rehab the property and would therefore only be worth paying $50,000. Sometimes you might even find a maximum allowable offer is actually a negative number meaning they would have to pay you to take the property off their hands! In such a situation, going through proper analysis helps you avoid the frustration of making an offer on a deal that would become a headache.

Propose:

This phase involves making an offer. Now that you've done a thorough analysis of the properties and you've found something you love (and the numbers make sense) there are a variety of ways you might make an offer. You can do it formally through an agent, in direct conversation with a seller or online through a real estate auction site. Regardless of the channel you use, if you want to buy a deal, you need to make an offer.

Once the offer is made, prepare for the rejection! As with anything else whether it's a job interview, prospecting or even trying to get a date, not everyone will accept the offer given. After all, you are dealing with human beings even in real estate, and they reserve the right to say no. Most of your proposals will probably never get accepted, and that's okay.

You must learn to love rejection and change your mindset around failure. Just because a deal doesn't go through or a proposal doesn't get accepted doesn't mean something is going wrong. Sometimes, it's for your own good. You might find rejection is just another stepping stone to something even greater.

For the offers that do get accepted; you now come one step closer to closing your first deal - our last phase in this funnel.

Success:

This is where you put the deal together, seal it under contract and do your best to ensure everything works well. Remember, in real estate, even if a deal is under contract, there's no guarantee that it's going to result in a closed deal. Although the bottom of your funnel is narrow and its purpose is to close the deal, you still need to be agile, open minded and vigilant because things rarely go according to plan.

In theory, you should be able to close on any deal once it's up and running, but we all know business isn't so black and white.

For example, I recently had to let go of a deal that didn't pan out because the seller withheld some pretty crucial information. I already put out the contract, and everything seemed to be going great, but I soon discovered the seller still had a mortgage on the property. He owed more money to the bank than I was paying him yet hoped the deal would go through without me noticing his bank debt.

So I packed up and moved on to the next offer that I was working on. This is the power of having a funnel that works. Of course, there's more to it than just this funnel but this is the process I have learned, and it seems to be the same process all the best real estate investors use to fill their pipeline with potential deals consistently.

Powerful tactics for finding great deals

Before we move on to the next chapter, I want to share some tactical examples of how you can literally find your next deals and fill up your pipeline fast.

1. Word of Mouth

The old fashion way is sometimes the best way. By letting everyone know that you are in the real estate business and that you're in the market to buy, you'll place yourself in the best position to find great deals. Networking with peers, joining your local real estate club or even online forums and marketplaces is a great start.

2. Newspaper

Although digital technology is taking over and hardly anyone uses traditional newspapers, the classified section of your local paper might still be a great place to start looking for homes that are for sale by owner.

Real estate agents usually also put their listings in the newspaper so it can be challenging figuring out what's also listed on the MLS and what isn't, but it's still a great starting point.

3. Multiple Listing Service

The Multiple Listing Service (MLS) is a collection of properties for sale by different real estate brokers across the country. When you go on sites like redfin.com or realtor.com, you'll be searching on the MLS, and the information found there is available for anyone to take advantage of.

4. Craigslist

Craigslist.org is a free classifieds website and one of the most popular sites in the world (number 51 to be exact). Millions of people are using Craigslist daily to buy, sell, trade or give away nearly anything you can think of under the sun. Real estate is no exception. If you know what you're doing, you could easily find some good potential leads within Craigslist.

5. Bank foreclosed property

You can easily get a great deal on foreclosed properties if you know how to do things right. Generally, these deals come about when a homeowner fails to pay a mortgage payment for an extended period forcing the lender to repossess the property and resell. Of course, it's sad for the homeowner who just lost the property, but once it's done, the property can become a great opportunity for you assuming the rehabilitation isn't too serious. Talk to your local real estate agent about foreclosures in your area and start checking some out. You might be surprised at the deals you can get.

6. Driving for dollars

Simply stated, this tactic involves you getting into your car and driving up and down the streets of neighborhoods you want to invest in, looking for potential deals. Usually, you want to focus on finding properties that seem vacant, distressed or transitioning negatively. For example, a property with 18" high grass is an indication that someone doesn't care about the property that much.

While driving down the neighborhoods you want to invest in, you'll likely encounter dozens of potential properties. Write down their addresses including notes about the condition of the place and take some photos as well. Then once home the real research begins. You might need to do some digging into the public records to find the owner of the property, or you might even do a reverse phone number search to the owner's number.

It's one of the lowest cost methods especially if you're just getting started and you're low on marketing or advertising funds. It also helps you understand the neighborhood better and of course the ultimate goal here is to capture as many raw leads so you can bring them into your funnel and eventually close the right deal.

7. Wholesalers

This is one of the best tactics to use especially if you already know a wholesaler. Wholesalers love putting deals together, and they already know creative ways of finding incredible deals so why not partner up with one?

For example, you can get a wholesaler to find a deal and put it under contract for $120,000 and then have them sell the agreement to you for $125,000, netting a $5,000 profit for himself/herself and enabling you to score a great deal in the process.

But you must find a good, trustworthy wholesaler. Finding a wholesaler isn't always easy but the more you network in your local marketplace and online, the easier it becomes. You could also train your own wholesaler who goes out and finds the deals for you.

8. Direct Mail

This is the act of sending out a large number of targeted letters or postcards to people who might be interested in selling their property, knowing that at least a small percentage might call you to talk more about the possibility and out of that small percentage, few will end up actually selling you their properties.

It's true none of us value direct mail anymore, but it isn't a lost cause. Sure it needs way more creativity and a solid plan backing this tactic, but if done right it can be a great way to generate great deals because most of the time, the people who will agree to sell you their properties are motivated sellers who don't want to deal with real estate agents. Direct marketing makes it easier for you to find an owner with a problem so you can help them solve it. It's not about tricking or taking advantage here, it's about building a reputation for yourself that you not only make money in real estate investing, you also help make a difference in people's lives.

There are many "lists" you can buy and mail to, but the most common is the "absentee list." This means that the person who is on record for owning the property doesn't live at the property. Companies like ListSource.com or MelissaData.com can help you find and purchase lists, and you can send letters, postcards or whatever creative method you prefer. The cost of sending a postcard is around $0.50 each, and a letter is about $1.00 each depending on how much work you do and how much you outsource.

It's important to mention that this tactic requires repetition. You can't just test this out once. Find a way to regularly reach out to the group you desire to connect with and build a rapport of some sort. And you also need to develop a brand and credibility both online and offline because the more your potential leads trust you, the easier it will be to strike a deal.

Chapter09: The Unsexy Stuff No One Likes To Talk About That You Need To Know About Before Your First Deal

Managing a full-time job and real estate.

More and more people with no prior real estate experience are quitting their jobs and going in full time to build their fortunes because as you might have guessed, it's not being viewed as one of the best ways to gain financial freedom. But not everyone should just quit their job. Sometimes, it's not even the right thing to do.

If you were wondering whether it is possible to keep your job and still grow a real estate business, then this chapter is for you. You can absolutely keep working a day job while expanding your portfolio.

In fact, one of the benefits of keeping your job and becoming a real estate investor is that you don't become dependent on it at the start. The cash flow generated by your new investments can go into exponentially growing your portfolio while you live off the salary from your day job. This can quickly fast track your business.

Having a stable income also helps with financing because banks will be more willing to help you out when you've got a credible 9-to-5. So if you already have a day job, don't just quit, there's much good that can come from it and you can already begin growing your portfolio by investing in a buy-and-hold deal with property management, partnering in a larger piece of property, investing in mortgages (notes) or serving as a private money lender.

There really is no right or wrong way to approach real estate as long as you have clarity on how much effort you're willing to put in. Whether you do it full time or part time you can still work your way into financial freedom. The most important thing is that you do a self-check and follow your gut when it comes to starting this. If you're unemployed, the choice is plain and clear, but if you currently have a job, please don't just quit because you hear people on YouTube advertising how they quit their jobs and made millions. You need to follow your own path and make informed decisions if you want this business to succeed.

That said, it's important also to emphasize that you can be able to figure this out on your own regardless of whether you do it full time or part-time. Real estate investing is not rocket science, and there are countless stories of average individuals who have self-taught themselves into vast fortunes.

A common question many new investors will ask is:

Do I need a guru to be rich?

The simple and short answer is absolutely not! You don't need a guru for anything really because you are the determining factor in your life.

Whether it's a health, relationship or financial goal, only you can make it happen. Oftentimes gurus are just external motivators.

However, I do recommend getting some kind of mentor. A mentor does not need to be a guru, and quite frankly I hope you get a mentor that isn't a guru because at least they will genuinely make time for you and help you walk this path of real estate investing without the hyperbole of fancy cars, models and getting rich quick. It is, in fact, true that there's a real estate guru trap you need to avoid, but that doesn't mean you shut out all experts. Some individuals are very knowledgeable and genuine, but you must do your homework and refuse to get caught up in the hype, empty promises, and wishful thinking.

How do you deal with expensive markets when starting out with no money

It's tough to start out in an expensive marketplace if you've got no cash in hand. There's no easy way around this. The best thing you can do is to get creative and innovative. Utilize the resources at hand, amplify your skills and use all the tricks, strategies and options I have detailed in this book. Without persistence, perseverance and lots of creativity, you just won't go very far regardless of the marketplace you're in. I have shared several strategies of how you can start small, how to find private money lenders or partner up with someone who has what you're lacking and you've read numerous stories of people who've been able to succeed even when the cards were stacked against them.

If your market is tough to crack and you really don't have the cash, consider the Turnkey investing option we talked about. But even then, do your due diligence and make sure it's right for you.

Before we move on, there's one more thing worth talking about that most skip over.

Getting an LLC. When should you get it and how do you start?

Many novice real estate investors are usually confused about getting an LLC, so it's only fair we touch on it here. And then you can make an informed decision over when you'll need one.

Not every real estate investor needs an LLC especially those just starting out, but of course, as your business grows it is advisable to get one.

A limited liability company is meant to protect you from potential lawsuits related to the property. Suppose you invest in a property, rent it to a tenant who decides to throw a big party, during which one of the tenant's guest falls over a balcony. If the injured guest pursued a claim based on the "unsafe condition" of the rental property, you would be named in the lawsuit. And you'd be forced to defend your personal assets (all of your personal assets), from the plaintiff's claims. If, however, a Limited Liability Company owned your property, your risk of exposure would be insulated by the protection of the company, leaving only the assets held by the LLC exposed to that lawsuit.

Nevertheless, the trouble of forming and maintaining a company may not be worthwhile protection anyway, especially if you breach some of the clauses (which will often happen for self-starters and small business owners who often co-mingle personal and business funds). There are other affordable options if you're just starting out that could protect you from the theoretical threat of a lawsuit. An example of this getting liability insurance.

Liability insurance is more affordable but beware, it has lots of carve-outs and limitations so take the time to understand exactly what you're getting by using this alternative option.

If you wish to minimize the risk, you just need to improve your chances of success by choosing the right strategy and complying with the corporate formalities required by applicable laws where you live, even if the steps are at times tedious and somewhat confusing.

If you are serious about building a future and a fortune in real estate, you should at least consider whether or not the acquisition through an LLC is the right choice for you. If so, it's better to start an LLC right off the bat as you make your first purchase instead of waiting to transfer the real estate to an entity at a later date where you might need more people involved (like your lender). An LLC doesn't necessarily offer any more or less protection from outside lawsuits than a properly formed and operated corporation or limited liability partnership, but it does provide enough benefits particularly for those just starting out.

To get started on your limited liability company I recommend following these five simple steps:

Step One: Choose Your State

As a new real estate investor, the best option is to form your limited liability company in the state where you live and where you plan to conduct your business. If you plan on investing in properties in different states, then you'll need to register for a foreign LLC in every state where you'll do business. You should know however that although business-friendly states like Nevada are great for registering your LLC, there's a lot of paperwork and extra fees involved.

Step Two: Pick a Name For Your LLC

Every state has its own rules about the kind of names an LLC can have. Do a name search online and learn about the laws in your state and pick a suitable name. Here are a few guidelines to help you get started.

- Your name must include the phrase "limited liability company" or one of its abbreviations (LLC or L.L.C)

- You may be required by some Banks or Attorneys to provide additional paperwork and have a licensed individual (doctor, lawyer, etc.) as part of your LLC.

- Your name cannot include words that could confuse your LLC with a government agency (FBI, Treasury, State Department, etc.).

Step Three: Choose A Registered Agent

The next thing you need is to appoint a registered agent (either a person or a business) that will send and received legal papers on your behalf. Official correspondence documents such as legal summons and registered filings will be received by your registered agent and forwarded to you.

Most states require every LLC to nominate a registered agent. This agent must be a resident of the state you're doing business in, or a corporation authorized to conduct business in that state.

Step Four: File Your LLC With The State

The fourth step you must take is to file your documents with the state. This is essentially how you create an LLC. This document is usually referred to as "Articles of Organization" or "Certificate of Formation" or "Certificate of Organization. Your LLC document is meant to outline the organizational structure of your business.

You'll also need to decide between appointing a manager for your LLC or have it be co-managed by the owners.

Step Five: Create An LLC Operating Agreement

The last step before you're ready to make your first purchase under your new LLC is to create an operating agreement. This is a legal document that outlines the ownership structure and member roles of your new LLC.

The good news is that most states in America don't have this as a requirement, but I still encourage you to create it anyways. Check in with your state to find out if it's mandatory. There are six main sections of an operating agreement.

- Organization - describing when and where the company was formed, who the members are and how ownership is structured.

- Voting and Management - addressing how the company is managed as well as how the members vote.

- Capital Contributions - covering which members financially support the LLC, and how more funds will be raised in the future.

- Distributions - Outlining how the company's profits and losses are shared among members.

- Membership Changes - Detailing the process for adding or removing members, as well as when members can transfer their ownership shares (if applicable).

- Dissolution - Explains the circumstances in which the LLC may be dissolved.

After following these steps carefully, you'll now be the owner of your very own LLC. After which you're ready to start growing your real estate business with more ease and peace of mind.

I do recommend also obtaining an Employer Identification Number (EIN) once you've formed the LLC. This is like a social security number for your LLC. And remember, you must separate your personal assets from your business, register your LLC for state taxes, set up accounting, and get yourself more protection with business insurance especially if you're going to be a landlord.

With all this knowledge in place, it's time to give you a simple process to help you go from ideation to your first purchase. As a beginner, if you do these four things diligently, you will close your first deal successfully.

The 4 steps to real estate success

The only secret sauce that will enable you to start winning with real estate from your very first deal.

• Find the deal

The first thing you need to do is find an incredible deal on a property that you love. If you don't love the property, don't invest in it. And the trick here is to find a deal that you love because the property resonates with you and the numbers are also good. You can't afford to compromise on either of this if you want to hit a home run.

How do I find the deal?

Well, I have shared so many tactics and ideas on where to start looking for deals in this book. Check in your local paper, visit trusted websites like Zillow go on MLS sites or call up real estate agents in the area you want to do business. If you are going to flip houses or do wholesaling, paid ads are also a great channel and when leveraged properly social media can bring you lots of leads with just a tiny budget.

Make sure you have your criterion clearly outlined when you start finding your deals.

Read through all the ideas contained in this book several times, test them out, drive for dollars if you have to, build relationships with real estate agents so they can keep you in the loop on hot deals.

Get creative and leverage social media and paid advertising if your budget allows. Whatever you need to do to always have a full pipeline of potential deals - do it!

Real world example:

Let's assume you live in Philadelphia and you've landed on an incredible 4-unit deal. This feels like the right fit for you. You have enough knowledge, and you've decided it's time to take the leap of faith and invest in your first property. The property is a 3,656 sqft that goes for $260,000, and since you're doing it as a private residential purchase, you can expect a down payment of 5%. Now it's time to talk about where you can get the money.

• Financing the deal

Most people think this is the biggest obstacle to closing that first deal, but in truth, it isn't. If you have an incredible deal finding the resources to make it happen won't be impossible. You can go to any American Bank to finance your deal. You can use one of the many alternatives I shared in the chapter on finance, and if you are going to live in one of the units (I highly recommend this strategy when getting started) then you can get an FHA (see glossary) so you can get the best loan with the lowest down payment.

How do I finance the 4-unit property that costs $260,000?

By living in one of the units, you could easily go to FHA and put 5% down which amounts to $13,000. Essentially, you'll be the owner of a property that's worth a quarter of a million dollars, yet you only invested $13,000 and if you can do the next steps right and hold on to this property long enough, in 30 years the property will be debt free, and it will have appreciated in value.

•Analyzing the deal

This is where you get to test and see if the 4-unit property makes sense to invest in. You must do a preliminary title search to ensure the property is good to invest and also to ensure it's worth the investment.

The most important thing when analyzing your first deal is to figure out whether the property is profitable in terms of cash flow. You also need to know if the numbers make sense in relation to cap rate; the internal rate of return and you must work out the cash flow before and after taxes. The mathematics doesn't need to be complicated or overwhelming. Keep it as basic as possible, use the formula outlined in the chapter on financing as well as the formulas I shared within the glossary. There are also many resources online like Biggerpockets.com that offer online calculators to help you analyze deals quickly.

Getting back to our 4-unit property, here are some basic calculations that would apply here.
Property = $260,000
5% down payment = $13,000 which means you need to finance $247,000. The debt that you'll need to pay annually can be rounded off to $15000. Annual income from this will be $34,200. The expense of maintaining this can

be assumed to be 50% of your income as a fair approximation, but since you're managing the property and fixing it, the cost should be lower. So let's assume this will cost you $12,000 annually. That leaves you with $22,200 - $15,000 = $7,200 positive cash flow which is about 50% ROI on your original down payment. Not too shabby for your first deal.

This is a fundamental example of how you must analyze your deals.

• Managing the deal

Assuming you're going to fix and maintain this first deal, the cost of repairing and running the place should be kept minimal, so it doesn't eat up on your profits.

How do I manage the deal?

To get the numbers I just shared above using that FHA loan, you need to fix and manage that property yourself. You also need to live in it for the first year. And you must continue paying yourself rent as well if you're a savvy investor. If you do your job right as a property manager, you could comfortably raise the rent on the property. Even as little as $50 per month annually, you'll be amazed how fast your income can grow over time. By now I am sure you can see that you don't need hundreds of thousands to start your real estate journey.

Chapter 10: Profitable Exit Strategies

Exit strategies are plans that smart real estate investors make to ensure they can exit a deal profitably. The correct approach will result in maximized profits and minimal risks, therefore, take your time making the decision on which strategy to implement.

What most successful real estate investors know that you don't:

Even the best real estate exit strategies can go wrong. They may not work, and you need to be prepared and counteract potential obstacles with multiple approaches.

A backup plan is critical, and you need to always have yours ready. Wondering what might go wrong with your exit strategy?

1. You might have unexpected maintenance costs that cancel out your profits.

2. You could get tenant issues resulting in lost rent.

3. You could struggle with management and end up with poor property management, which can diminish the value and hurt potential cash flow.

4. You might experience a distinct lack of demand, failed escrow or the backing out of a lender, which may hinder the flipping of a property.

5. Depreciation may occur.

And these examples don't even begin to cover the long list of what could go wrong. I say this to make you aware of the fact that you need to be prepared for anything. One exit strategy is never going to be enough. That's why I am sharing several!

Here is a list of exit strategies you should consider until you find what's the right fit for your particular deal.

Prehabbing

This exit strategy is actually a hybrid combining rehabbing and wholesaling. During pre-hab, minimal work is done (as opposed to flipping where lots of rehab work is done), to bring the property up to selling quality. This option is great if you're a DIY type of real estate investor, but you don't want the full commitment required in a fix-and-flip deal. Simple ways you can pre-hab a property includes updating the landscape, replacing the carpet, doing a new paint job on the interior and exterior, etc.

Prehabs are usually not difficult, and they are inexpensive, and they are often limited to improvements that do not require a professional.

Flipping

This is one of the most popular and arguably most profitable real estate exit strategy because it will allow you to sell the target property at full market value. The formula for success when it comes to flipping a deal involved finding a property at under market value in a market where demand is strong, putting together a reliable team of contractors, sticking to the rehabilitation budget and timeline and then finally selling the property quickly to the highest offer possible. Rehab requires you to purchase a house, fix it and then sell it for more than the original investment cost, which includes purchase, and repair costs. There are so many factors to consider when doing a flip so make sure you learn as much as you can about flipping houses and real estate markets beforehand to avoid significant loses.

Wholesaling

When starting out with little to no cash (which is what this book has focused on), this might be one of the best exit strategies to implement. You (the investor) will necessarily act as the middleman between a motivated seller and an end buyer. Your role here will be to find and quickly sell a property for a respectable profit margin.

You have two ways of doing this:

You can sell or "assign" your purchase contract to an end buyer, or you can actually close on the property and immediately resell the property to another investor in what's known as a "double close."

The best part about this strategy is that you don't need to invest any personal cash in facilitating this deal and you'll instead make money via your wholesaling fee. Many new real estate investors prefer this strategy because it really is the easiest way to get started.

Lease Option

This exit strategy is more commonly known as rent-to-own, and it will allow you to rent out the property to a tenant, but with the option to purchase at a later date. Usually, an agreement will be made between you and the tenant for a rental period, after which they can begin the purchase process. Once the rental period ends and the tenant decided to move forward with the purchase, their monthly payments will then be made toward the purchase of the property (similar to mortgage payments). The payments are made directly to you instead of a lender.

Seller Financing

This is an innovative technique that permits the owner to sell the property to a buyer. If you choose to use this as your exit strategy then essentially you would (as the owner) finance the deal and act as the bank. Then you will receive monthly payments. As the seller, you will be required to maintain the mortgage loan to cover the sales price and the reason it works so well is because of the flexibility it provides to both buyer and seller. You wouldn't need a middleman or financial lender and the closing process is swifter. It also helps your listings stand out in the market since you'll be allowing buyers to finance the purchase through you.

It's also worth mentioning that seller financing can also create a good source of monthly income and it spreads out tax requirements as well (if done correctly).

As a buyer using seller finance, one of the key benefits is being able to negotiate to put little to no cash for down payment, and it enables you to buy more properties without affecting your credit report.

Buy and Hold Real Estate

The example I shared in the previous chapter is a perfect example of investing in a property that could have a buy-and-hold exit strategy. Once you have the property and have a positive cash flow, you could choose not to sell it and instead receive the money cash flow for as long as possible. This strategy however always includes some rehab work on the property to increase the value, quality and market price of the asset. You will be able to raise rental rates and build up equity in an asset with this exit strategy. However, it comes with its fair share of headaches and responsibilities as you manage the property.

Bank Owned Homes

A bank owned home or real estate owned (REO) is a property that is being sold by a lending institution such as a bank.

When a foreclosure happens on a property, the financing entity will seize it back into their possession and sell it under market value to a new buyer. Since it's expensive for banks to hold and maintain these properties, it's in their best interest to sell them as soon as possible and to do so they will usually remove any outstanding liens and debts from the property. Bank owned homes are usually sold through real estate auctions or through the lender's special REO listing website.

Please note this isn't a standard exit strategy and certainly not easy to use as a novice real estate investor but with time and experience you can to navigate real estate auctions and leverage this strategy to get some great deals.

As an investor I expect you to delineate between each of these options based on your desired outcome. The strategy you choose will depend on the amount of cash you want to invest and your level of experience. There's no wrong or right way of doing this, but the more educated you are about your options, the easier it will be to navigate the deal and find the most profitable exit strategy.

Chapter11: Growing Your Empire

Once you've successfully executed on your first few deals and you get some momentum going, you can start scaling your real estate business. Start small, grow steadily and scale it exponentially at the right time. Don't try to skip over the learning curve.

Your education and the experience you get starting with a basic 2 - 4 unit property and building toward larger units until you are ready for commercial real estate is priceless. Honor the journey, embrace and enjoy the process. The hustle, dedication, patience, and persistence you put into this will be richly rewarded as you watch your wealth and real estate portfolio grow over the next few years. It doesn't really matter how you start. Whether you have some cash in hand or no money at all, you are now fully equipped to make something happen.

No more excuses.

If you genuinely want financial independence and you want to retire early and focus on things that matter to you then now is the time to take action in that direction. Remember not to compromise on your cash flow especially in the beginning when you're laying the foundation for success. If a property isn't producing at minimum 5% cash flow, keep looking until you find that first deal that will set you up for success. Before evaluating future projections, value adds, location and so on make sure the numbers are right and that you get positive cash flow out of the investment.

While our journey in this book might be coming to a close, your journey into real estate success is just beginning. Take what you've learned here, implement, experiment, network with others in your space who are doing well and keep running toward your dream.

Before we part ways, let me share a full glossary of real estate terminology you need to know as well as resources that will help you with your continued education.

Full Glossary:

Accrued Interest

Accumulated interest earned or due but not yet paid

Acre

A measure of land equaling 43,560 square feet.

Adjusted Cost Basis

For accounting purposes, this is the original cost plus improvements minus depreciation or cost recovery taken.

After-Tax Cash Flow

Effective gross income minus operating expenses and debt service plus or minus any tax savings or liability.

Agency

A relationship of trust whereby one part (the principal), entrusts another party (the agent) to act in their behalf and to represent them in doing business with other parties.

Alligator

A property that has a negative cash flow.

All-Inclusive Trust Deed (AITD)

The borrower obtains a new mortgage, which is structured to include the old mortgage. The borrower makes payments on the new mortgage directly to the lender, who makes payments on the old first mortgage.

Amortization

A method of gradually paying off principal on a mortgage. Each payment reduced (amortizes) the original amount.

Amortized loan

A loan in which the principal, as well as the interest, is payable in monthly or other periodic installments over the term of the loan.

Administrator

A party appointed by a court to administer the estate of a person who has died without leaving a will.

Annuity

A payment of equal installments paid periodically for a given number of periods.

Appraisal

An estimation of the value of real property at the present time or past date, never future. Any of the three methods are used where applicable.

a. Cost approach

b. Income approach.

c. Market data approach.

Appraiser

A disinterested party who evaluates a property and determines its value.

Appreciation

A property's growth in value.

Arrears

The payment of money after the fact. Interest and taxes paid in arrears would represent money paid for a period gone by.

Asking Price

This is the price an appraiser has determined for a property and the price for which it is on the market.

Assessed Value

This is the value as determined by the local tax assessor's office to levy local taxes.

Assessment

This is the value set on a property by the local government for the purpose of real estate taxes.

Asset

This is any possession of value that an individual owns which may be used for payment of a debt.

Assign

To transfer one's rights in a bond, lease, mortgage, or other legal instruments to another person.

Assuming Mortgage

This is the taking of title to a property by a buyer, whereby he or she assumes payment of note or bond secured by a mortgage against the property.

Balance Sheet

This is a financial statement showing assets, liabilities, and net worth.

Balloon Payment

A large financial payment due on a note, usually after partial amortization of the debt through installment payments.

Bankruptcy

Proceedings against a debtor, who has been declared legally insolvent, to distribute the debtor's property among the creditors.

Binder

This is a small deposit of money paid with a temporary agreement to purchase property under specified terms.

Bird Dog

A person who is on the lookout for properties that are for sale.

Blanket Mortgage

One mortgage that covers several different parcels of real property.

Blended Interest Rate

This is the interest rate resulting from half the difference of the interest rate initially written for the mortgage and the current market rate of interest.

Book Value

The value of property carried on a company's books. It is usually the cost minus depreciation or cost recovery plus capital additions.

Bond

This is the evidence of a personal debt, which is secured by a mortgage on real estate.

Broker

This is a state licensed agent who represents buyers and sellers in real estate proceedings.

Brokers price opinion

This is the opinion of a Real Estate Broker as to the value of a property (like a "lite" appraisal) often abbreviated as BPO.

Capital

This is the money used for investment purposes.

Capital Gains

This is the profit realized above the adjusted cost basis on the sale of a property.

Cash Flow

This is the effective gross income minus operating expenses and debt service.

Caveat Emptor

This is Latin for "let the buyer beware." The buyer must inspect the goods or property and purchase at their own risk.

Chattel

This is personal property.

Chattel Mortgage

A mortgage on a personal property.

Closing

This is the procedure whereby the property title is conveyed from seller to buyer.

Collateral

Real or personal property pledged as security for repayment of a loan or debt.

Commission

This is usually a percentage of the purchase price paid to the broker or agent for services rendered.

Condemnation

This is the process by which property of a private owner is taken, with or without consent, for the public use. Fair compensation must be paid.

Condominium

Individual ownership of an apartment and an undivided interest in the common areas and facilities, which serve the multi-unit property.

Contingency

A possible event based on the happening of an uncertain future event.

Contract

An agreement between competent parties in the performance of a legal consideration, whereby each party obtains a right to what the other wants.

Contract For Deed

A contract for the sale of real property wherein the seller is obligated to provide a merchantable title after the buyer has paid for the property, usually in installments. Commonly abbreviated as CFD. Also called Land Contract (LC) or Agreement for Deed (AD).

Contract For Purchase And Sale

An agreement between buyer and seller for real property to transfer title to that property at a future time for a specific sum of money.

Conveyance

The transfer of real estate from one party to another.

Cooperative

An apartment house or similar property owned in corporate form by all the tenants. Each has stock in the corporation, which owns the building.

Covenant

Insertion of a written agreement into deeds and other documents promising performance of certain acts, or stating specific uses of real estate.

Cow

This is a term used to describe an income property with a high positive cash flow.

Creditor

The lender. The one to whom the debt is owed.

Cure Date

The last day given for bringing mortgage payments current at the beginning of the foreclosure process.

Dead Asset

This is an asset that an investor does not want (in the investor's eyes it has no value).

Debt Service

The sum of the annual principal and interest payments expressed as a percentage of the amount owed.

Deed

A legal document, which conveys real estate from seller to buyer when properly, executed.

Default

Failure to discharge a duty or meet your obligation.

Deficiency Judgment

A judgment rendered in court for the difference in the amount realized at a foreclosure sale and the amount owed by the mortgagor, if the foreclosure sale fails to liquidate or satisfy the debt entirely.

Depreciation

This is the decline in property value due to obsolescence, natural wear, age, or any other condition.

Discount

This is the percentage of the original balance of the loan that is charged the borrower. Sometimes referred to as points. It's also the difference between the selling price of a mortgage and the amount due.

Discounting A Note

This is the process of offering a promissory note for less than its face value to enhance its marketability.

Distressed property

This is a bargain property that is substantially below its present or projected renovated value.

Duplex

This is a two family home where the units share a common divider and are situated either side by side or up and down.

Earnest Money

This is a deposit of money given by a party to bind the contract usually credited toward the sales price.

Effective Gross Income

This is the difference between the total gross income and vacancy allowance.

Effective Interest

This is the interest rate the borrower actually pays as opposed to the nominal interest rate. The effective interest rate is made higher than the nominal rate by addition of points or discounting a loan.

Eminent Domain

This is the power of the government to take private property for public use in return for fair compensation. This power is exercised through condemnation.

Encroachment

An obstruction or building, which intrudes upon or trespasses upon the property of another.

Encumbrance

This is anything that mars title to a property such as a mechanic's liens, lien for back taxes, an unpaid mortgage, judgment, etc.

Equity

This is the value of a property minus the debts or liens against it. It increases in margin over the years as the mortgage is paid off.

Escape clause

A clause added to the contract that allows either party the option of exiting the contract. Both parties are no longer bound by any contractual obligations.

Escrow

Funds held by a third party to be released when certain conditions are in a contract are fulfilled.

Estate

Ownership interest in real property.

Estate by the entireties

Ownership by husband and wife with the right of survivorship.

Estoppel Letter

A letter certifying the exact balance of a mortgage or another loan at a given time.

Exchange

This is the exchanging or trading of a business property you own for another trade or business property that is like it. No taxes are due in such an exchange under a given set of circumstances.

Exculpatory clause

This is a clause in a contract relieving one of the parties of personal responsibility or liability.

Expenses

The cost of maintenance, repairs, and rental costs that are deducted from a property's gross income.

Extension Clause

This is a clause contained within some lease option contracts that provides for the terms under which the contract may be extended.

Face Value

This is in reference to a note. The face value is the full amount for which the note has been written.

Fair Market Value

This is the appraised value of a property as compared with other property values on the market.

Flipping

The turnover of a property. This is where an investor buys a property to sell it for a profit immediately.

Fiduciary

An agent in the position of confidence to his principal. It's also a relationship of trust and confidence imposed by law.

Financial Analysis

This is an investor's determination of the value of a property according to their specific needs.

Financial Leverage

This is the use of other people's money for investment purposes.

Financing

This is the way in which an investor obtains the capital with which to purchase a property.

First Deed Of Trust

This is a deed of trust recorded first. Equivalent to a first mortgage.

Forced Sale

This is the sale of a property used as security for a loan to repay the creditor, or others, in the event of default on the loan.

Foreclosure

A legal procedure where the lending institution or agency sells the property because the borrower is in default of the payment terms of the mortgage.

General Partnership

This is a form of business where two or more individuals enter into an agreement to conduct business. Profits and losses are shared in a predetermined fashion, and all partners are jointly and severally liable for debts of the general partnership.

Grace Period

Additional time granted to perform an act or make a payment before default.

Grandfather clause

Properties that do not conform to current ordinances, regulations or codes, but are allowed to continue to be occupied because the properties predate the institution of the ordinances, codes, and regulations.

Grantee

This is a person or entity that is receiving interests or rights of real estate. For example, a buyer.

Grantor

This is a person or entity that conveys their interests or rights in real estate. For example, a seller.

Gross Income

This is the total income from a property before the deduction of expenses.

Gross Income Multiplier

This is the number which when multiplied times the gross number, would give an indication of property value. It is strictly a guide.

Homestead Exemption

This is protection extended by the law preventing the forced sale of an owner-occupied dwelling by certain creditors.

Homestead Tax Exemption

This is the credit against taxes given in some states to individuals who own and occupy a dwelling and to certain other individuals including disabled veterans, those over 65 years old, widowed, or handicapped.

Installment Loan

This is a loan that must be repaid in no less than two payments. A loan of six months or greater is preferable when establishing credit.

Installment Note

This is a note, which specifies how mortgage payments will be made, when they will be due and for what amount.

Installment Sale

This is a sale whereby (for income tax purposes) it is not taxed totally in the first year of the sale. For this to be valid, there must be a minimum of two installment payments over two tax years.

Instrument

A written legal document delineating the rights of the parties.

Interest Rate

An amount a borrower must repay in addition to the full amount of the loan.

Intestate

An individual who has dies without leaving a valid will.

Involuntary lien

A lien, like real property tax liens, which are recorded against the property without the consent of the owner.

Instant Equity

The difference between the property's value and what you paid for it.

Joint Tenancy

Ownership of real estate by two or more persons, each of whom has an undivided interest with the right of survivorship.

Joint Venture

An arrangement where two or more individuals or corporations join together on a single project as partners.

Jointly and Severally

This is a legal term indicating that two parties have entered into a contract and the two parties are not only liable together but individually as well.

Judgment

This is the verdict of a court on a matter presented to it. A money judgment dictates that a party must make payments to another to settle a claim.

Junior Lien

This is a mortgage or other encumbrance with a secondary interest. A lien junior to another mortgage or lien.

Lease

A contractual agreement between the owner and the tenant, which allows the tenant the use and occupancy of the property for a specified period of time. A lease is an encumbrance against a title and gives the tenant an actual interest in the property for years.

Lease Option

This is an agreement between two parties where the party that owns the property extends the right to purchase the property at a future date. The second party lives in the property until the lease option expires. Commonly abbreviated as LO or L/O.

Leasehold

The estate or interest held by the lessee in the property of another.

Legal Description

This is the means to identify the exact boundaries of a property. A surveyor will use the recorded plat method, metes, and bounds method or the government survey method to describe a real property.

Lessee

An individual who contracts to hold occupancy rights in the real estate property of another.

Letter Of Credit

This is a letter usually from a financial institution, guaranteeing a debt incurred by a third party.

Letter of Intent

This is a letter stating a buyer's intent to make an offer to acquire a specific property. It is not a binding contract.

Leverage

This implies obtaining a higher return on borrowed money than the cost of borrowing it. It's a situation where the smallest amount of cash is invested in obtaining the best yield, percentage-wise.

Lien

This is a claim lodged against real estate to effect repayment of indebtedness. For example, a mechanic's lien, where the contractor records his or her lien for work done and not paid for.

Limited Partnership

This is a partnership composed of a limited partner and a general partner. The limited partner contributes capital but is not liable for any debts of the partnership, nor can they manage or control the partnership.

Listing

This is an agreement whereby the owner of a property gives a real estate agent the right to handle the sale, lease of property and to receive a commission for this service.

Marketable Title

A title free and clear of liens and encumbrances that might be objectionable.

Market Value

This is the highest price for a property that a buyer is willing to pay and the lowest prices that a seller agrees to accept.

Mechanics Lien

A lien existing in favor of mechanics, suppliers or other persons who have supplied materials or performed work in connection with the construction or rehabilitation of a building.

Mete

Measures such as inches, yards, miles or feet.

Metes And Bounds

A description of the boundary lines of land, setting forth the boundary lines within their terminal points and angles.

Moratorium Of Interest

A time during the term of a loan wherein no payment of interest due is made.

Mortgage

This is a legal document that conveys title to real estate as collateral for the payment of a debt.

Mortgagee

The lender of money who holds a mortgage on a property as security for repayment of the loan.

Mortgagor

The borrower of money who gives a mortgage on a property as collateral for repayment of the loan.

Mortgage Commitment

This is a formal notice from a lending institution stating the amount it will lend for the purchase of the property.

Multiple Listing Service

This is a multi-realty service whereby members of the local Board of Realtors exchange their listings.

Negative Cash Flow

This is a property that costs you money instead of making your monthly income.

Net Income Approach

This is a technique used to evaluate larger properties to determine their value. It is done by calculating the net income they produce.

Net Listing

A price under which an owner will not sell the property. The broker is entitled to the excess over the net listing as his commission.

Net Net Net (Triple Net Lease)

An agreement, which specifies that the tenant pays real estate taxes, insurance and all maintenance, costs of the property.

Net Operating Income (NOI)

This is the gross income minus any operating expenses. Debt service is not deducted as an expense and therefore not included here.

Net Spendable Income

This is the amount remaining after expenses and debt service and any taxes due have been deducted from the gross income.

No Doc Loan

This is a loan where the borrower is not required to present any documentation to secure a loan.

Non-Owner Occupant (NOO)

This is a property where the owner does not live. Generally refers to rental property.

Note

This is the legal evidence of debt.

Option

An instrument giving the right to a party to lease or purchase the property over a specified time period for detailed consideration. It is binding for the optionor but not the optionee.

Optionee

The person who has the legal right to purchase or not purchase a specific property in the future.

Optionor

The seller of a property who extends an option to someone else. If the optionee exercises the option, this person is legally bound by the contractual obligations. If the option is not exercised, then the optionor is released from any responsibilities.

Owners Of Record

This is a record of all the owners that are listed on a deed. It is recorded in the county courthouse.

Package Mortgage

This is a mortgage, which in addition to encumbering real property also includes personal property such as a dishwasher, refrigerator or oven.

Partnership

Two or more people associated for the purpose of carrying on business activities.

Pay Down

This is the amount of principal on a loan retired through payments at a given time.

Personal Property

All property besides real property.

Plat Book

A public record containing maps of land showing the division of such land into streets, blocks and lots. It also includes measurements of individual parcels.

Points

An originating fee or a percentage based on the amount of mortgage money advanced, to be paid by the seller.

Positive Cash Flow

This is when rental and other income exceeds all of the costs and expenses of ownership.

Preliminary Title Search

This is the first review of all previously recorded documents regarding a specific property, to make sure that property may be sold.

Premium

This is an additional sum of money paid as an incentive for someone to do something.

Prepayment Clause

This is a clause in a mortgage giving the mortgagor the privilege of paying off the mortgage before its due date.

Principal

This is the sum of money used as funds for the investment.

Promissory Note

This is usually a note given to the seller by the buyer, which promises to pay back principal to the seller. It also states the interest rate and the timeframe for payback.

Pro Forma Statement

This is a financial statement based on anticipated, not actual income and expenses.

Pro Rata

Buyers and sellers portion of prepaid or unpaid expenses such as real estate taxes.

Purchase Money Mortgage

These are funds advanced in the form of a mortgage by the owner of the real estate to the buyer for the purpose of buying their property.

Quit Claim Deed

A deed transferring whatever interest in the property that the grantor may have and is commonly used to clear title.

Real Property

Land, and generally any improvements added to the land.

Real Estate Owned (R.E.O)

These are properties that financial institutions have repossessed as a result of default on a mortgage and which these institutions (such as banks), are willing to sell.

Recording

The act of entering in the public record any instrument affecting title to real property.

Release Clause

A statement in a blanket mortgage that allows a specifically described parcel to be released from under the blanket lien after a sum of money is paid, or a period is up.

Reproduction Cost Analysis

This is a technique used to evaluate a property by estimating the cost of building the same or similar structure, adding the cost of land and subtracting an allowance for wear and tear.

Sandwich Lease

While having the option to buy a property, the investor subleases it to gain positive cash flow.

Security Deposit

This is the amount of money paid by a tenant before moving into the premises to cover any damage incurred while living there, or to protect the landlord in the event that the tenant leaves without being current on rent payments. If the tenant is current and the unit only has a reasonable amount of wear and teat, then the deposit is generally refunded.

Subject To

This is a term that means "buying a property with an encumbrance in place." In Real Estate Investing, it is generally a method of buying a property without getting new financing. Buying a house with a mortgage in place. Commonly abbreviated as Sub2, Sub-2, Sub To and Sub-To.

Survey

This is a map prepared by land engineers or surveyors indicating the location and boundaries of the property described in the title.

Tax Certificates

These are bonds sold to recoup unpaid property taxes by the country in which the property is located. When the property is auctioned, the certificate holders may either use the certificates as money to bid on the property or redeem them for face value plus interest.

Tax Sale

The sale of a property because of a delinquency in the payment of taxes.

Tenant

A person having the temporary use and occupancy of real property owned by another.

Terms

The exact way a property will be purchased.

Testate

An individual who dies leaving a valid will

Tile

A legal document certifying the right of ownership or property.

Title Insurance

Insurance issues by a guarantee company protecting the property owner against any flaws in the title that might affect ownership or potential losses.

Title Insurance Company

A business that reports on the status for the title on a specific property and whether or not it has any liens against it. After this title search is completed, the company will issue a deed to be signed by all the owners of the property, which should be notarized and recorded in the public records.

Title Search

This involves the investigation of title records; history of previous ownership to ascertain if liens, encumbrances or other outstanding claims exist that may prevent legal conveyance of title.

Township

This is a unit of measure used in the government survey method of land description equal to 36 sections, which is 36 square miles.

Unilateral Contract

This is a contract in which one party is bound by another to do something. If the second party chooses to exercise the contract, the first party must perform any contractual obligations that the party may have. If the second party chooses not to exercise the contract, the first party is released from any contractual obligations.

Unsecured Line Of Credit

This is a credit history developed by an individual who borrows small amounts of money, which do not require collateral.

Usury

This is a rate of interest on a loan, which is greater than the law allows.

Vacancy Rate

This is an estimate of the amount of time the rental property will be vacant multiplied by the rental rate of the unit(s). The amount is used in estimating the investor's value of an income property.

Violation

An act, deed or creation of a condition that violates the law in the use of the property.

Warrant

To guarantee something to be as represented.

Win-Win

A solution to both seller and buyer needs.

Wraparound Mortgage

A mortgage held by the seller-mortgagee. The buyer-mortgagee pays the seller-mortgagee the debt service on the wraparound mortgage, and the seller-mortgagee continues to pay the debt service on the underlying or original mortgage.

Zone

An area designated by the authorities for a specific use, subject to certain restrictions.

For more resources on real estate here are some recommendations.

1. Bigger Pockets -

https://www.biggerpockets.com

2. National Real Estate Investment Group (Investing Education) - https://www.nreigrp.com/blog/

www.ingramcontent.com/pod-product-compliance
Lightning Source LLC
Chambersburg PA
CBHW071543210326
41597CB00019B/3107